OLD TESTAMENT SERMONS

Robert Murray M'Cheyne

OLD TESTAMENT SERMONS

Edited by
Michael D. McMullen

THE BANNER OF TRUTH TRUST

THE BANNER OF TRUTH TRUST
3 Murrayfield Road, Edinburgh EH12 6EL, UK
P.O. Box 621, Carlisle, PA 17013, USA

*

© Banner of Truth Trust 2004

ISBN 0 85151 873 7

*

Typeset in 11 /15 pt Goudy Old Style BT at
the Banner of Truth Trust, Edinburgh.
Printed and bound in Great Britain
at the University Press,
Cambridge

DEDICATION

I dedicate these volumes to three American Christian families that my wife and I met in Scotland and grew to love in Christ. In no order other than alphabetical, they are Roy and Marcelle Ciampa and their children; Thor and Li Madsen and their children; and Terry and Denise Wilder and their children. In the Lord's gracious plan, Drs Ciampa, Madsen, Wilder and I are all now serving Him as Seminary Professors in America.

MICHAEL D. MCMULLEN

Contents

Publisher's Note — viii

1. God's Care for the Animal Creation (*Num.* 22:32) — 1
2. The Cities of Refuge (*Josh.* 20) — 9
3. The Waters Are Come In Unto My Soul (*Psa.* 69: 1–3) — 19
4. I Will Praise Thee (*Psa.* 86: 12–13) — 29
5. By the Rivers of Babylon (*Psa.* 137) — 39
6. Things That Must Be Done Now (*Eccles.* 9:10) — 45
7. His Name Shall Be Called Wonderful (*Isa.* 9:6) — 50
8. God's Twofold Dealings with Natural Men (*Isa.* 28:14–18) — 57
9. For the People Shall Dwell in Zion (*Isa.* 30:19–21) — 67
10. The Day of the Great Slaughter (*Isa.* 30:25–26) — 76
11. The Silence of Christ (*Isa.* 53:6) — 83
12. Delighting in the Sabbath (*Isa.* 58:13–14) — 89
13. The Spirit of the Lord Is upon Me (*Isa.* 61:1–2) — 98

14. The Harvest Is Past, the Summer Is Ended
    (*Jer.* 8:20–22)   102

15. Give Glory to the Lord (*Jer.* 13:15–17)   113

16. Can Thine Heart Endure? (*Ezek.* 22:14)   123

17. The Way Hedged Up (*Hos.* 2:6)   135

18. O Israel, Return (*Hos.* 14:1–6)   139

19. Trust Not in a Friend (*Mic.* 7:5–7)   150

20. A Pure Language (*Zeph.* 3:9–11)   155

21. The Candlestick and the Olive Trees
    (*Zech.* 4:2–6)   159

22. Not by Might, Nor by Power (*Zech.* 4:6)   167

23. The Lord Hearkening to His People (*Mal.* 3:16)   171

Publisher's Note

This is the first of three volumes of 'new' sermons by the nineteenth-century Scottish preacher Robert Murray M'Cheyne, who died in 1843 at the early age of 29. Most of the sermons have not previously been published, though a few were in print for a time in nineteenth-century editions. They were transcribed from M'Cheyne's manuscript notes in New College, Edinburgh University, by Michael D. McMullen, Associate Professor of Church History in Midwestern Baptist Theological Seminary, Kansas City, Missouri, and have been only lightly edited.

May these sermons, fragrant with the sweetness of Him whose Name is as ointment poured forth, bless a new generation of readers and preachers in the twenty-first century!

1

God's Care for the Animal Creation[1]

And the angel of the LORD said unto him, Wherefore hast thou smitten thine ass these three times? Behold, I went out to withstand thee, because thy way is perverse before me (Num. 22:32).

BALAAM WAS AN UNCONVERTED MAN, and the chief feature in his character was the love of money. He 'loved the wages of unrighteousness' (*2 Pet.* 2:15). Other wicked men, it is said, 'ran greedily after the error of Balaam for reward' (*Jude* 11). Another feature of his character was cruelty. He regarded not the life of his beast, for the tender mercies of the wicked are cruel (*Prov.* 12:10).

When the ass saw the angel of the LORD and turned out of the way, this might have wakened him to think that *he* was surely going out of his way; but no, instead of wakening his conscience, it wakened his anger. He smote the ass to turn her into the way.

Again when the ass saw the angel of the LORD a second time, she crushed Balaam's foot against the wall. This might have wakened him to think that this journey was only to bruise himself;

---

[1] Preached in St Peter's, Dundee, March 1837.

but no, instead of wakening his conscience, it only wakened his anger, and he smote her again.

Again when the ass saw the angel a third time, she fell down under Balaam. This might surely have wakened him to think that this journey would end only in his destruction; but no, his conscience was unawakened, his anger was kindled and he smote the ass a third time with a staff.

And now God opened the ass's mouth to plead with him. But even this did not move him. His anger only became more ungovernable. 'I would there were a sword in mine hand, for now would I kill thee' (*Num.* 22:29). But God can restrain man's wrath. The angel now appears to Balaam and pleads the cause of the dumb beast, 'Wherefore hast thou smitten thine ass these three times?' (verse 32). He shows him that his anger was most unjust and most unreasonable, that the ass had really been the means of saving his life; for, 'unless she had turned from me, surely now also I had slain thee, and saved her alive' (verse 33).

Thus will God one day plead the cause of all dumb animals. He is now counting the blows which wicked men give to their injured cattle and will one day demand it of them. 'Why hast thou smitten thine ass these numerous times?'

The doctrine I would draw from this account is this:

GOD IS MUCH DISPLEASED WITH THE SIN OF CRUELTY TO ANIMALS.

God is Himself kind and merciful to the lower animals. This may be proved in a great many ways.

1. It may be proved from their state in paradise.

i. *In paradise God made them all very good.*

God's Care for the Animal Creation

When the creatures came from the hand of God they were all good. Even in the eye of God, who must surely be the best judge of happiness, their condition was good and happy. Men sometimes wonder how under the government of a good and gracious God the beasts should be so pained and burdened as they are now. But you should remember that when God created them, they were not as they are now: poor and burdened and diseased. There was not one among them sickly or lame or broken or driven away. For the Great Shepherd looked over all, and even He said that all was good, VERY GOOD!

ii. *In paradise animals were submissive to man.*

You remember how lovingly they all came flocking round our father, Adam, to see what names he would call them. How even the monarch of the woods came, 'cowering low' at his feet. And the eagle came down from his nest in the rugged rocks above. All came acknowledging man as his lord and master. They were, though, kind and friendly to one another. There were no brutal wars then, no bull fights then. The wolf did not carry off the bleeding lamb. The hawk did not pounce upon the timid sparrow then.

The pictures which the prophets give us of the second paradise which is yet to come, seem to be borrowed from the first paradise, for then, 'The wolf also shall dwell with the lamb, and the leopard shall lie down with the kid; and the calf and the young lion and the fatling together; and a little child shall lead them' (*Isa.* 11:6).

iii. *In paradise the beasts were not to be slain.*

The shedding of blood was a thing unknown in those happy days. Man lived on the herb of the field and the fruit of the tree. The dismal scenes of the slaughter-house were all unknown in paradise. Not even in sacrifice were the beasts to be slain. Man had not sinned, no death had been incurred, and therefore no beast needed to die. In all this was shown that God Himself is kind and merciful to the lower animals. Now, brethren, you may be harsh and cruel to the poor dumb animals if you will, but look to God and you will see nothing but kindness and mercy toward them.

2. It May Be Proved from Some Facts in History.

i. *At the Flood.*
When God brought the Flood upon the world of the ungodly, destroying all the wicked men whom He had made, preserving only eight persons in the ark, how kindly and graciously did He preserve vast multitudes of the lower animals! How kindly did He gather them two and two of every kind into the ark, and laid up sufficient food for them all, and shut them in. And all were kept safe and quiet for so long a time. This was a wonderful instance of God's kindness to the lower animals, when so many thousands of men perished in the waters.

ii. *In this story of Balaam.*
How wonderfully did God interpose on behalf of the injured animal! It was the Angel of the Lord, or rather the Angel Jehovah, none other than the Eternal Son of God, who stood with the flaming sword. Twice did he stand by and see the prophet cruelly beat his ass. But when the prophet smote a third time with the staff, then He who delighteth in mercy could stay no longer. He opened the dumb ass's mouth. 'The dumb ass speaking with man's voice forbad the madness of the prophet' (*2 Pet.* 2:16).

And when even that would not do, then does that blessed Saviour take up the cause Himself, 'Why hast thou smitten thine ass these three times? Unless she had turned from me surely now also I had slain thee and saved her alive.' He showed that the life of the innocent ass was more valuable in his sight than the life of the wicked prophet. How plain brethren, that though man may be cruel yet God is merciful and kind to the lower animals.

iii. *In God's treatment of Nineveh.*

When the men of Nineveh repented at the preaching of Jonah, and God repented of the evil and spared the city, then it displeased Jonah exceedingly and he was very angry and said, 'It is better for me to die than to live' (*Jon.* 4:3). Then did God plead with the angry prophet, 'Should not I spare Nineveh, that great city, wherein are more than sixscore thousand persons that cannot discern between their right hand and their left hand, and also much cattle' (verse 11).

The flocks and herds of mighty Nineveh sent up a cry into the ears of the God of hosts. And that was one reason why He spared the place. Oh! brethren, you may beat and injure poor dumb creatures if you will, but remember that God delights not in cruelty to the animals. He never afflicts willingly even the beasts that perish.

3. IT MAY BE PROVED FROM THE LAW OF GOD.

It is written in the Law, 'Thou shalt not muzzle the ox when he treadeth out the corn' (*Deut.* 25:4). How plainly does this prove that God takes care for oxen. Again it is written three times over, 'Thou shalt not seethe a kid in his mother's milk' (*Exod.* 23:19; 34:26; *Deut.* 14:21). How plainly did God wish to show that He delighteth not in even the appearance of cruelty. Again it is written, 'Thou shalt not see thy brother's ass or his ox fall down by the way, and hide thyself from them: thou shalt surely help him to lift them up again' (*Deut.* 22:4).

Oh! brethren, you may think the pains and sorrows of the beast that falls beneath its burden unworthy of a moment's thought, but does not that prove how unlike you are to the God who delights in mercy? For He pleaded for the fallen beast, even from the mountain top of Sinai.

Again it is written, 'If a bird's nest chance to be before thee in the way in any tree, or on the ground, whether they be young ones or eggs and the dam sitting upon the young, or upon the eggs, thou shalt not take the dam with the young: but thou shalt in anywise let the dam go . . . that it may be well with thee, and that thou mayest prolong thy days' (*Deut.* 22:7).

Ah, brethren, think of the God who made planets and worlds, who calls all the stars by name, who reigns over thrones and dominions and principalities and powers, yet making a law for the poor bird that makes its nest of straws upon the ground, and then think if He be not a God that delighteth in mercy!

And last of all, it is written, 'Remember the sabbath day to keep it holy. Six days shalt thou labour and do all thy work: but the seventh is the sabbath of the Lord thy God: in it thou shalt not do any work, thou, nor thy son, nor thy daughter, thy man servant nor thy maidservant, *nor thy cattle*' (*Exod.* 20:8–10). Does God take care for cattle? Yes, brethren, even for cattle does our God care! Even for them has He provided a Sabbath, a day of rest.

And if any man or any set of men do in express contradiction to the eternal Law of God give their sanction and countenance to Sabbath labour, they only show how different their mind and spirit is from the mind of God. Oh, brethren, have nothing to do with laying Sabbath labour upon man or upon beast, or be sure that God will one day require it at your hands. For He is a just God as well as a merciful God. He delighteth in justice, and He delighteth in mercy.

4. It May Be Proved from the Providence of God.

And here I would answer a very common objection. You may say, God is not kind and merciful to the animals, else why do they suffer at all? They never sinned, and is it not very cruel, instead of kind, that they should be afflicted with pains and disease and death?

To this I answer: As long as this was a sinless world there was no pain among the animals. All was life and health and enjoyment. But when man fell, it pleased God to show the exceeding hatefulness of sin by involving all the creatures in his Fall. The very earth was cursed with barrenness for man's sake. A blight has come over its loveliest seasons and thorns and thistles grow in the richest gardens.

The creatures too were cursed for man's sake. They left the green herb to devour each other, and now disease and pains and death make their hideous ravages among them. 'For we know that the whole creation groaneth and travaileth in pain together until now' (*Rom.* 8:22).

Yes, brethren, and God means that every groan of the suffering animal should ring through your hearts and make you feel, 'This is the misery of sin.' But still, though this be a fallen world, and though the curse has spared nothing that is of the earth, still, just as, in spite of the barrenness, there are scenes of surpassing loveliness and skies that might almost have hung over paradise, just so, in spite of the curse that is on the creatures, there are kind providences toward them which show that God is the same God that ever He was, a God that delighteth in mercy!

'Are not five sparrows sold for two farthings, and not one of them is forgotten before God?' (*Luke* 12:6). 'Consider the ravens, for they neither sow nor reap; which neither have storehouse nor barn; and God feedeth them' (*Luke* 12:24).

'Wilt thou hunt the prey for the lion? or fill the appetite of the young lions' (*Job* 38:39). But God provides for them: 'The young lions roar after their prey, and seek their meat from God' (*Psa.* 104:21). 'These wait all upon thee; that thou mayest give them their meat in due season' (verse 27). 'Thou openest thine hand, and satisfiest the desire of every living thing' (*Psa.* 145:16).[1]

---

[1] The notes of this sermon are incomplete. We have no way of knowing how M'Cheyne would have concluded, but it seems certain that he would have made a powerful application of his text to the consciences of his hearers.

2

The Cities of Refuge[1]

The LORD *also spake unto Joshua, saying, Speak to the children of Israel, saying, Appoint out for you cities of refuge, whereof I spake unto you by the hand of Moses: that the slayer that killeth any person unawares and unwittingly may flee thither: and they shall be your refuge from the avenger of blood. And when he that doth flee unto one of those cities shall stand at the entering of the gate of the city, and shall declare his cause in the ears of the elders of that city, they shall take him into the city unto them, and give him a place, that he may dwell among them. And if the avenger of blood pursue after him, then they shall not deliver the slayer up into his hand; because he smote his neighbour unwittingly, and hated him not beforetime. And he shall dwell in that city, until he stand before the congregation for judgment, and until the death of the high priest that shall be in those days: then shall the slayer return, and come unto his own city, and unto his own house, unto the city from whence he fled.*

And they appointed Kedesh in Galilee in mount Naphtali, and Shechem in mount Ephraim, and Kirjath-arba, which is Hebron, in the mountain of Judah. And on the other side Jordan by Jericho eastward, they assigned Bezer in the wilderness upon the plain out of the tribe of Reuben, and Ramoth in Gilead out of the tribe of Gad, and Golan in Bashan out of the tribe of Manasseh. These were the cities appointed for all the children of Israel, and for the stranger that

---

[1] Preached in St Peter's, Dundee, 15 April 1838.

sojourneth among them, that whosoever killeth any person at unawares might flee thither, and not die by the hand of the avenger of blood, until he stood before the congregation (Josh. 20).

WHEN ISRAEL TRAVELLED forty years in the wilderness, they had many types of the Saviour constantly before their eyes. When a believing Israelite went out in the morning, when the desert was all glistening with dew, all round about the camp there lay a small round thing, white like hoar frost, beautiful to look upon. It was the manna that came down from heaven to nourish Israel. And his heart leaped within him as he gathered, for he thought of the heavenly manna which God would send in the latter day.

When he stood beside the smitten rock and saw the waters gush out and follow them day by day, a mighty river running through a desert, he thought with joy of the Saviour who is 'as rivers of water in a dry place' (Isa. 32:2).

As he lay waking in the night-watches, he might often look through the curtains of his tent upon the bright pillar of fire that gave them light all the night long, and he would think of Him who is a covering to the soul, and the light of the world. 'When I sit in darkness, the LORD shall be a light unto me' (Mic. 7:8).

Or when the wicked Israelites were bitten with serpents and the brazen serpent was lifted up, oh, with how full a heart he would gaze upon it and think on the Saviour yet to be lifted up!

When Israel came into the land of promise these types of the Saviour were withdrawn. The manna ceased to fall with the early dew. The water no more followed them. The pillar-cloud retired into the Holiest of all. But God provided new types of the Saviour. Of these none was more singular than the Cities of Refuge. Oh, it is sweet to think that many an Israelite indeed was led by these to Jesus, the true City of Refuge.

The Cities of Refuge

Many an aged Israelite sat in the cool of the day beneath his vine or his fig-tree and after singing some Songs of David, the sweet singer of Israel, would point his children to the distant hill with the refuge-city smiling on its brow, and tell how to flee from the wrath to come.

The cities of refuge were intended to set forth Jesus.

1. THEY WERE LIKE CHRIST IN SITUATION.

i. In Their Nearness

If anyone will examine a map of the Holy Land, he will find that these six cities were chosen on account of their central situation. Three of them are on one side of the Jordan, and three of them are on the other side. Two of them are in the utmost north, two in the middle and two in the south, so that there was no place in the whole land of Israel where an Israelite would be more than half a day's journey from one of the cities of refuge. So that he might say of it what Lot said of Zoar, 'Behold now, this city is near to flee unto, and it is a little one: Oh, let me escape thither . . . and my soul shall live' (*Gen.* 19:20).

So is Christ. He is a near Saviour. He is not far from any one of us. Awakened souls always think that salvation is far from them. Alas, they say, I have a great deal to do before I can be a saved person! They 'go about to establish their own righteousness'. But what says the Bible? 'Say not in thine heart, Who shall ascend into heaven? (that is, to bring Christ down from above:) or, Who shall descend into the deep? (that is, to bring up Christ again from the dead.) . . . The word is nigh thee, even in thy mouth, and in thy heart' (*Rom.* 10:6).

Oh! dear souls, 'the word is nigh thee'! Christ is in the Bible, the Bible is in thy hand; nay, Christ is nearer still: the word concerning

Jesus is in thy mouth. Oh, let him be nearer still! Let him be in your heart. Believe on the Lord Jesus, and thou shalt be saved. 'Behold now, this city is near to flee unto.' Escape thither, and thy soul shall live.

ii. In Being Conspicuous

Nothing is more remarkable about the cities of refuge than the conspicuous situations which they occupied. All of them except one were situated on high hills; and a city that is set on a hill cannot be hid.

a. *Kedesh in Galilee.*

This was in mount Naphtali. It stood eminent upon a hill and commanded the whole of populous Galilee. A plain stretched from it for eight miles as far as the Sea of Galilee. And on the other side it commanded the plain as far as Carmel and Mount Tabor.

b. *Shechem in Mount Ephraim.*

This city lay between two remarkable hills, both of which can be seen at a great distance, as they rise 800 feet above the plain.

c. *Kirjath-arba, which is Hebron in the mountain of Judah.*

This city of refuge was still more remarkable. It is built upon the slope of a hill and the hill over it commands a view of the whole country as far as the Dead Sea. It was from this that Abram saw the smoke of the country go up like the smoke of a furnace.

d. *Bezer in the wilderness upon the plain.*

This is the only city of refuge that was not on a hill. But still it was abundantly conspicuous, for there was no hill near it, nothing to distract the eye, till it caught upon the towering walls of Bezer in the wilderness, glittering in the sun.

The Cities of Refuge

e. *Ramoth in Gilead.*

That this city was high and lifted up, we know from its very name, for Ramoth in the Hebrew tongue means 'high places', and you remember how the false prophets said to Ahab, 'Go up to Ramoth-gilead, and prosper: for the LORD shall deliver it into the king's hand' (*1 Kings* 22:12). It commanded all the plain of Jordan eastward.

f. *Golan on the hill of Bashan.*

This city was as remarkable as the others. The hill on which it stood is celebrated for its height. 'The hill of God is as the hill of Bashan; an high hill as the hill of Bashan' (*Psa.* 68:15).

In the case of every one of these cities, then, we find that it was easily seen. Indeed, it seems probable that there was scarcely a place in the whole land from which you could not spy one of these refuge cities. So that, when the believing Israelite went out to meditate like Isaac at eventide, when he saw the sun gleaming on the fruitful top of Gerizim, or the white walls of Hebron, or the far-off tower of Bezel in the wilderness, or the embowered dwellings of Ramoth-gilead, or the snow on the high hill of Bashan, every one seemed a witness for Christ. Every one had a tongue and said, 'Come unto me, and I will give you rest.'

Dear brethren, Christ is a lifted-up Saviour. As Moses lifted up the serpent in the wilderness, so the Son of Man has been lifted up on the cross, that whoever looks to Him may be saved. His word is, 'Look unto me, and be ye saved, all the ends of the earth' (*Isa.* 45:22).

Some anxious souls say, 'I fear Jesus does not wish to be my Saviour, or God is not willing that I should flee to Him.' Ah, look here, see how these refuge cities were lifted up. Just so is Christ. For what end? That there might not be a trembling soul in the whole land unconverted; that whosoever believeth in Him should not perish. This shows the heart of God toward you. He wants you to come to a lifted-up Christ on the cross and on the throne. Christ is a lifted-up Saviour in the preached Word, that any sinner may flee to Him and be safe. Oh! come to a lifted-up Christ!

2. THEY WERE LIKE CHRIST IN EASE OF ACCESS.

I would speak of the *roads*, the *waymarks* and the *open gates*.

i. THE ROADS

The way to the cities of refuge was prepared. We are told by the Jewish Rabbis that they were always kept in good repair, very wide and level and easy, that the manslayer might flee without hindrance. And it seems probable that the prophets allude to this when they speak of a highway through the desert, as in Isaiah 35:8: 'An highway shall be there, and a way, and it shall be called The way of holiness.' And again, 'Go through, go through the gates; prepare ye the way of the people; cast up, cast up the highway' (*Isa.* 62:10). And to this, perhaps, Jesus alluded when he said, 'I am the way . . . no man cometh unto the Father, but by me' (*John* 14:6).

Ah, dear brethren! The way to Christ, the true refuge, is wide and open. There is no hindrance, 'a fool cannot err therein'. A little child can find nothing to stumble over. Yea, a little child travels it best. Oh! flee from the wrath to come, and flee to Jesus!

ii. WAYMARKS

The Rabbis also tell us that there were waymarks placed here and there along the road, pointing to the refuge; and perhaps there is allusion made to this fact in Jeremiah 31:21: 'Set thee up waymarks, make thee high heaps.' So it is with Christ. Along the road, how

The Cities of Refuge

many waymarks point to the Refuge! The Bible is the great waymark, and it all points to Jesus. Moses, Psalms, Prophets all point to Jesus the Lamb of God. Godly friends, they too are waymarks, pointing you with affectionate hands and drawing you to the Saviour. Ministers are waymarks set high up, to cry aloud day and night, witnesses for Jesus to cry, 'How shall you escape, if you neglect so great a salvation?' Escape for thy life, look not behind thee. Tarry not in all the plain. Dear friends, if you perish it is because you are determined to perish.

iii. OPEN GATES

We are told that the gates of the cities of refuge were open both night and day. The gates of other cities were shut every night and opened in the morning. But the Refuge had open gates continually. To this Isaiah perhaps refers, 'Therefore thy gates shall be open continually (*Isa.* 60:11); and John in Revelation, 'And the gates of it shall not be shut' (*Rev.* 21:25). So it is with Christ. He is open to receive sinners night and day. Nicodemus came to Him by night and found him an open Saviour. Come early or come late, you will find an open Jesus. 'Those that seek me early shall find me' (*Prov.* 8:17). The thief on the cross found Christ at the last hour.

When He was on earth, you remember how often He went into the temple early in the morning and taught the people, saying, 'I am come a light into the world.' He stood till evening and, as the sun was setting, said, 'Yet a little while is the light with you. Work while ye have the light.' On the last day of the feast Jesus stood and cried, 'If any man thirst, let him come unto me' (*John* 7:37). 'All day long I have stretched forth my hands unto a disobedient and gainsaying people' (*Rom.* 10:21). No one ever came to Jesus and found the door shut: 'He that cometh unto me I will in no wise cast out' (*John* 6:37).

3. THEY WERE LIKE CHRIST IN THE SAFETY FOUND THERE.

i. Safety Was Obtained at the Entering of the Gate (*Josh.* 20:4). As long as the manslayer was only upon the road to the city, he was not safe. The avenger of blood might overtake him and kill him. But the moment he set his foot within the gate of the city he was safe.

So is it with a sinner in Christ. As long as you are only anxious about your soul, you are not safe. The broken law follows hard after you. Your past sins cry loud against you. Conscience throws fiery darts after you. You flee; still you are not safe till you are in Christ. But 'if I may but touch the hem of His garment I shall be made whole'. Ah, yes! One step within the Refuge and you are safe. One grain of faith as small as a mustard seed will give peace to the soul. And oh, what peace there is in being safe, safe for time and safe for eternity!

My dear friends, you may say what you will of the joys of sin, of the pleasures of company and the table and the game, there cannot be true rest in them, for there is no safety. 'There is no peace, saith my God, to the wicked' (*Isa.* 57:21). Oh, flee into this strong tower and be safe! Oh, if you could taste for half an hour the peace of being forgiven, of having a clean conscience, of being in Christ, all the pleasures of sin would lose their sweetness. You would say, No, I have strong consolation for I can flee for refuge to the hope set before me. Now I count all things but loss that I might win Christ and be found in Him. There is no condemnation to them that are in Christ Jesus!

ii. Both Jew and Stranger Found Safety (*Josh.* 20:9).
The cities of refuge were 'for all the children of Israel, and for the stranger'. Oh, there is something sweet and pleasant in that word,

The Cities of Refuge

'Whosoever', for it includes men of every country, of every age, of every sin. So free is Christ, the true Refuge. The gospel is 'the power of God unto salvation to every one that believeth; to the Jew first and also to the Greek' (*Rom.* 1:16). 'Whosoever believeth on Him shall not perish' (*John* 3:16) 'Whosoever will, let him take the water of life freely' (*Rev.* 22:17). Dear brethren, the refuge city invites you, however deep you have waded in sin, however long you have despised the Saviour. 'As I live, saith the Lord GOD, I have no pleasure in the death of the wicked . . . turn ye, turn ye . . . why will ye die?' (*Ezek.* 33:11).

iii. INSTRUCTION WAS TO BE FOUND THERE.
From the next chapter (*Josh.* 21) we learn that these six cities were among the cities given to the Levites. Now we know that the Levites were the public teachers, that they taught the people to read and understand the Word of God. So that when a poor manslayer fled to the refuge he found kind instructors ready to teach him the Law of his God.

So is it when we fly to Christ. He gives us the Spirit of truth to lead us into all truth. And we have an unction from the Holy One and know all things. 'I will pray the Father, and he shall give you another Comforter, that he may abide with you for ever; even the Spirit of truth; whom the world cannot receive.' 'The Comforter, which is the Holy Ghost, whom the Father will send in my Name, he shall teach you all things and bring all things to your remembrance, whatsoever I have said unto you' (verse 26). Dear brethren, hereby ye may know if you are within the refuge or no. 'If any man have not the Spirit of Christ, he is none of his' (*Rom.* 8:9).

But there are dangers to take heed to:

a. *Some awakened persons seem to be seeking Christ in a very slack way.* You seem to be sitting down by the way, loitering and taking a little pleasure and ease by the way, some turning back. Ah, dear souls, you are not safe yet! The Avenger is close behind you, you are not safe till you are within the refuge, and you may never be there. Up and flee! Tarry not in all the plain. Remember Lot's wife. She fled out of Sodom, not into Zion!

b. *Some Christians seem unconcerned to abide in Christ.*

Some who seemed to close with Christ seem now not to care so much about it, and not to be in earnest to abide in Him. Read with me Numbers 35:26–28: 'But if the slayer shall at any time come without the border of the city of his refuge, whither he was fled; And the revenger of blood find him without the borders of the city of his refuge, and the revenger of blood kill the slayer; he shall not be guilty of blood: because he should have remained in the city of his refuge until the death of the high priest: but after the death of the high priest the slayer shall return into the land of his possession.'

Now then, dear souls, abide in Him. Every branch that beareth not fruit he taketh away. 'If ye continue in my Word then are ye my disciples indeed.' With full purpose of heart, cleave unto the Lord. 'Little children, abide in him; that when he shall appear, we may have confidence, and not be ashamed before him at his coming' (*1 John* 2:28).

3

The Waters Are Come In Unto My Soul[1]

Save me, O God; for the waters are come in unto my soul. I sink in deep mire, where there is no standing: I am come into deep waters, where the floods overflow me. I am weary of my crying: my throat is dried: mine eyes fail while I wait for my God (Psa. 69:1-3).

THIS PSALM IS QUOTED many times in the New Testament, and four of these times it is applied to our Lord and Saviour Jesus Christ.

1. When Jesus was explaining to His disciples that they would be hated by the world even as He had been, he said, 'But this cometh to pass, that the word might be fulfilled that is written in their law, They hated me without a cause' (see *Psa.* 69:4).

2. When Christ found in the temple those that sold oxen and sheep and doves, He made a whip of small cords and drove them all out of the temple; and then His disciples remembered this Psalm, 'The zeal of thine house hath eaten me up' (verse 9).

---

[1] Preached in St Peter's, Dundee, 9 December 1838.

3. When Paul, in Romans 15:3, would persuade the Christians not to please themselves, but every one his neighbour, he points to Christ as described in this Psalm. 'For even Christ pleased not himself; but, as it is written, The reproaches of them that reproached thee fell on me' (*Rom.* 15:3; see *Psa.* 69:9).

4. In that hour of unspeakable agony when Christ hung upon the accursed tree, His heart turned upon this wonderful Psalm. 'Jesus knowing that all things were now accomplished, that the Scripture might be fulfilled, saith, I thirst' (*John* 19:28). And they filled a sponge with vinegar and put it on a hyssop reed and put it to his mouth; so the word was fulfilled, 'They gave me also gall for my meat; and in my thirst they gave me vinegar to drink' (*Psa.* 69:21).

You are to look upon this Psalm then, dear brethren, as upon a repository of the mind and heart of the Saviour. Here you will find some of His deepest and most unutterable experiences. The true and only meaning of this Psalm is to unfold and open out to your view the bosom and heart of the Son of God in his dark agonies, when He who was our Surety died. Those were the very feelings of His heart. We see here:

1. THE SUFFERINGS OF ALL WHO DIE WITHOUT CHRIST.

All these words, we see, described accurately and faithfully the sufferings of Him who stood as the Surety of sinners. He was infinitely holy in Himself, and infinitely dear to God, and yet, because He stood in the room of sinners, you see how much He suffered. It is a lamentable fact that, although this glorious Surety is offered to sinners, the most of the men and women in the world die without embracing Him as their own. They die to bear their own sins and we may see here, as in a glass, the misery into which they fall.

The Waters Are Come In Unto My Soul

The waters are come in unto my soul (verse 1):
We do not know, in the history of the Saviour's sufferings, whether there was any sudden plunge into the deep ocean of affliction. These words seem to point to such a thing, as if God had cast Him suddenly into the deep waters; as Jonah was lifted up and cast into the raging sea; and as in Psalm 102, 'Thou hast lifted me up, and cast me down' (*Psa.* 102:10). It is the cry of one who feels the sudden penetrating gush of waters closing in around them on every side, 'Save me, O God; for . . .'.

So it will be with all Christless persons. 'Their foot shall slide in due time' (*Deut.* 32:35). At present they are greatly at ease. Scripture and experience both testify that Christless persons are at ease till they die.

In the vision in Zechariah 1, the horses say, 'We have walked to and fro through the earth, and, behold, all the earth sitteth still, and is at rest' (*Zech.* 1:11). 'I have seen the wicked in great power, and spreading himself like a green bay tree' – or like a tree that grows in its native soil, that has never been transplanted (*Psa.* 37:35). 'There are no bands in their death: but their strength is firm. They are not in trouble as other men; neither are they plagued like other men' (*Psa.* 73:4–5). Such, I suppose, is the state of almost all Christless persons here this day. They are sitting quiet and are thinking in their seats. They are at ease in Zion. They are like wine settled on its lees. How sudden, how dreadful, how overwhelming will the plunge into an undone eternity be. This is the cry that will burst out from their soul, 'Save me, for the waters are come in unto my soul.'

Just as when a ship is sailing at night before the wind – there is a gentle ripple on the sea, the sailors are gone to rest, they have gentle dreams of home and friends – when suddenly the ship strikes on a sunken rock. The sailor wakes at the vessel's sudden roll. And the gush of the waters is in his soul. So sudden is the destruction of Christless persons. They are brought into desolation as in a moment. I do feel that most of you are saying, 'Peace and safety', when sudden destruction is coming like travail on a woman with child, and you shall not escape.

I sink in deep mire where there is no standing (verse 2):
This shows that the Saviour felt His troubles increasing upon Him. He felt the darkness becoming greater and greater. He was like one sinking in mire. Friend after friend forsook Him. Enemy after enemy came upon Him. Wrath came upon Him to the uttermost. Such will be the lot of all Christless souls. When they die, they fall into increasing troubles. They sink in deep mire where there is no standing. This teaches us:

a. *They will turn more wicked every day.*
Just as wicked men on earth grow more wicked every day, so will wicked men in hell. They gnaw their tongues for pain and yet blaspheme the God of heaven because of their pains, and so they will sink deeper and deeper in the mire where there is no standing.

b. *Their sufferings will be eternal.*
It is possible that some souls, when they first drop into hell, will try to keep up their cheerfulness. They will hope that it may soon be over; but ah, when they find out that it is eternal, that the pit is bottomless, they will sink and sink in deep mire where there is no standing. When the sailors at Greenland were enclosed by the ice for so long a period, at first they tried to keep up their hearts by hoping that they would yet be set free. But when month after month rolled over them and still the ice enclosed them in frozen sorrows, and when their food was daily growing less and less, their minds began to sink and sink in gloom and despair. This is a faint picture

of the sinking of a lost soul when it finds out that hell is eternal punishment. 'I sink in deep mire.'

When the Saviour said, 'I am come into deep waters, where the floods overflow me' (verse 3), He felt that He was under a load of waters which he could not lift from Him. He felt like Jonah: 'The earth with its bars is about me for ever.' Such will be the feeling of Christless souls. At present they have slight views of God's anger against sin, but then they will know what the deep floods are. They will feel like Cain, 'My punishment is greater than I can bear.'

c. *God has forsaken them.*

This was the very point and sting of the Saviour's agony, 'My God, my God, why hast thou forsaken me?' This will be the very hell of hell. At present God has not forsaken Christless persons. His hand preserves your body every day. His pleasant sun shines upon you. He makes the rain to fall in your service. He makes food to nourish you and water to drink. He gives you his Bible, and his striving Spirit. Oh, no! You are not yet forsaken by God. But when you die, if you die Christless, you will be utterly and eternally forsaken by God. You will be weary with your crying, your throat will be dried. No Father's hand will preserve you. No pleasant sun will shine upon you. No rain will fall for you. No meat will nourish you, no drop of water will cool your tongue. God's children will have His smile upon them, His arms around them, but you will wait in vain for a kind look. His eye will not pity. His hand will not spare.

Oh, be warned to flee from the wrath to come! 'If they do these things in the green tree, what will be done in the dry?' If you saw a green tree cast into a great furnace and you saw it burnt up, flaming and crackling, and if I asked you now what would become of a dry tree, a withered log, if it were cast in there: 'Ah,' you would say, 'the withered log will go up in a blaze.' Now Christ was the green tree and you are the dry tree. Flee from the wrath to come!

2. THE GREAT LOVE OF CHRIST TO SINNERS.

You hear people often talking about the great love of Christ to sinners, and yet it appears to me that most people have no idea of what the love of Christ is. You will see it if you meditate on that word in verse 2, 'I am come into deep waters, where the floods overflow me.' It was of His own free will that He came. 'No man taketh [my life] from me, but I lay it down of myself. I have power to lay it down, and I have power to take it again' (*John* 10:18). Just as Jonah said, 'Take me up, and cast me forth into the sea', so did the Saviour give himself into the hands of sinners. 'I am come into deep waters.' Consider two things:

i. THE PLACE HE LEFT.
a. *He was in riches and in glory.*
Some of you know how hard it is to part with a little money. How hard it would be to lay aside a handsome fortune, to leave a great house and lands and become a poor man. Yet this Christ did. He was rich, and for our sakes He became poor. He had all the riches of heaven at his command, and yet see what deep waters He came into. He became a worm, and no man. He made his cradle in a manger, He slept on a pillow. He had not where to lay His head.

b. *He was in honour and reputation.*
Some of you know how hard it would be to lay aside the admiration and praise of good men. But to leave all your friends and go away to a foreign shore for thirty years, to be of no reputation! Yet Christ did this in an incomparable manner. He was in the form of God and thought it not robbery to be equal with God, yet He became of no reputation and took on Him the form of a servant. 'I am come into deep waters.' How much love there is in that little word.

c. *He was beloved.*

Some know how hard it would be to break away from the bosom of a father you love; to leave a home where you had been brought up and where you were daily their delight, to go into a world where all would oppose you and be enemies to you. This did Christ! He was in the bosom of God. He was by Him as one brought up with Him. He was daily his delight, rejoicing always before Him. Who can tell the infinite ocean of joy that was poured from the bosom of the Father into the bosom of the Son in that Eternity that is past? Yet all this He left to come into deep waters! Herein is love!

ii. For Whom He Came.

a. *For those who were without strength, sinners, ungodly.*

It is a very difficult thing to do a kindness to a person whom you, in your heart, condemn. When you believe a person to be a bad man, it is very difficult to treat them with kindness, or to deny yourself to do them a favour. Yet this is what Christ did! He hates sin. He is angry with the wicked every day. He has created an eternal hell to show His utter abhorrence of sin, and yet He came and died for the ungodly.

b. *For His enemies.*

It is still more difficult to do a kind thing to those who are full of rage and enmity against us. If you know a man who is not only wicked but who hates you and is full of rage against you, it is a difficult thing to love that man's soul and to suffer some pain in order to do him good. Yet this is the love of Christ. He came to a world of enemies. He laid down His life for those that hated Him, that preferred a robber to Him, that wagged their heads at Him, that gave Him vinegar, that crucified Him. 'Herein is love, not that we loved God . . .' (1 John 4:10). 'I am come into deep waters.'

This truth is of use to draw sinners to Jesus Christ. I have shown you your sad condition. Now here behold the way of safety. You are every moment exposed to the wrath of God, and yet you are every moment exposed to the love of the Saviour. This love does not regard them as good and holy, but as ungodly, as sinners, as enemies. You always think that you must repent and mend your life to make yourself worthy of the Saviour's compassion. Learn that the Saviour came for the ungodly, for those who are not repenting, nor believing. 'If any man hear my voice . . .' 'This is the record that God hath given to us, eternal life.' Oh! If God would take away the blindfold that is over your eyes, then the light of the glorious gospel would shine unto you. 'But if our gospel be hid, it is hid from them that are lost.'

3. THE PERFECT SAFETY OF ALL WHO HAVE TAKEN REFUGE IN CHRIST.

The words of our text describe the sufferings of our Lord and Saviour Jesus Christ. These sufferings are all past. He has suffered them all. The cloud has spent all its lightning upon His head. The storm has spent all its fury against Him. The floods have rolled over Him and are gone for ever.

i. THESE SUFFERINGS WERE ALL IN THE STEAD OF OTHERS.

If He had had any sin of His own, He must have suffered on account of it. But He had none. He knew no sin, but was made sin for us. On Him were laid the iniquities of us all.

ii. ALL WHO TAKE HIM AS SURETY HAVE FULLY SUFFERED IN HIM.

They will never suffer any more. 'Through this man is preached unto you the forgiveness of sins.' These are the very sufferings they deserve, but they have been borne by the Lamb. 'Comfort ye, comfort ye my people, saith your God. Speak ye comfortably to Jerusalem, and cry unto her, that her warfare is accomplished' (*Isa.* 40:1–2).

4. APPLICATION.

i. Some awakened soul among you may say, 'My sins are so many, so abominable, so daring against God, against conscience, against the Bible, that I fear the floods will come in unto my soul.' Now, if you are willing to take Christ as your Surety, you do not need to be afraid. He offers Himself to you, for He offers Himself unto all men. If you take Him, it matters not whether your sins be many or few, for the infinite floods went over Him. He suffered as much as God thought fit to pour upon Him.

ii. Some of you close with Christ, and yet dare not say that your sins are forgiven you. Now, this is wrong. If you do, as a hell-deserving sinner, look to Him as your Surety, then your peace should be like a river. Take the peace of it. It is no presumption to feel safe when you fly to Jesus Christ. It is no presumption in the chickens to feel safe when they flee under the wings of the hen. It was no presumption in Noah to feel safe when he fled into the Ark. It was honouring the Word of God.

It is no presumption in you to feel divine peace when you take Christ as your Surety, for in Him you have borne all – the waters of wrath have already come in unto your soul. You have already sunk in deep mire, you already know what it is to be forsaken of God in your Surety. There is now no condemnation to you that are in Christ Jesus. Let your peace be like a river. The soul that is in Christ should be in the smile of a pardoning God. 'Be of good cheer: thy sins are forgiven thee.'

iii. Some of you have many doubts and fears. Abide in Him. 'If ye continue in my word, then ye are my disciples indeed; and ye shall know the truth, and the truth shall make you free.' Remember, it is simply looking as a sinner to that divine Surety that gave you peace at first, that will give you peace to the very last. If you would have calm, steady, abiding peace, and if you would have holiness springing up in your heart, keep an eye upon Christ wading through His Father's wrath for you. Your warrant to believe in Him is two-fold:

a. That you are a lost sinner.

b. That He freely offers Himself to every sinner.

Be often at Gethsemane. Be often at Golgotha. The tree of a sinner's peace grows best when it is planted near to the cross. 'He that hath the Son hath life.'

4

I Will Praise Thee[1]

I will praise thee, O Lord my God, with all my heart: and I will glorify thy name for evermore. For great is thy mercy toward me: and thou hast delivered my soul from the lowest hell (Psa. 86:12–13).

THERE IS NO DUTY more frequently spoken of in the Psalms than the duty of praising God. 'Is any afflicted? let him pray. Is any merry? let him sing psalms' – this seems to have been the constant rule in the heart of David, the sweet singer of Israel. In the time of affliction, when waves and billows went over him, he prayed. When God answered his cry and brought him up into the light of his countenance, then he would burst into a song of praise.

'My heart is fixed, O God, my heart is fixed:
I will sing and give praise.
Awake up, my glory; awake, psaltery and harp:
I myself will awake early' (*Psa.* 57:7–8).

Just so it was here. He began in sorrow. 'Bow down thine ear, O LORD, hear me: for I am poor and needy.' But his sorrow was turned into joy, and he ends with praise. 'I will praise thee, O Lord my God,

[1] Preached in St Peter's, Dundee, May 1837.

with all my heart: and I will glorify thy name for evermore.' There are two things to be discovered in these words.

The first is *the sincerity of his praises*. He calls God his God. Some men praise others before they have become acquainted with them but here David calls God his. He is not a stranger.

The sincerity of his praise is also seen in that it is 'with all my heart'. It is a complete affection, the whole heart is engaged with it. And then also it is 'for evermore'. It is no transient admiration, but for evermore. Death shall not interrupt this praise. The song begins on earth, and it shall know no end in glory.

Secondly, observe that *these are not groundless praises*. He assigns a reason for them. 'For great is thy mercy toward me: and thou hast delivered my soul from the lowest hell' (verse 13). God had mercy on his soul; therefore David praised Him. God had spared him long, waited on him, brought him to close with Christ; therefore did his heart rejoice, and he could not keep in his praises. Out of the abundance of the heart, the mouth spoke: 'I will praise thee . . . and I will glorify thy name for evermore.'

The doctrine I would gather is this, *Whenever God saves a soul that soul becomes a praising soul.* Notice then:

1. UNAWAKENED SOULS DO NOT PRAISE GOD, NOR GLORIFY HIM.

As long as a man is unconcerned about his soul so long is he without praise.

i. *He does not praise God in his heart.*

He has no thankful remembrance of the love of God to lost sinners, nor of the sufferings of Christ, nor of the power of the Holy Ghost. An unawakened man never had so much as one admiring thought of God or of Christ.

ii. *He does not praise God with his lips.*

He never sings the praises of God heartily in the house of God or in his family or in his secret retirement. Perhaps he may love the music, but he does not love the praise. He spends none of his time in praising God.

iii. *He does not praise God with his life.*

He does not glorify God. He lives only for his own glory, that men may praise him, but he never does anything in order that God may have the praise. He eats and drinks only for his own nourishment and enjoyment. He does not eat and drink to the glory of God.

QUESTION: Why is this?

ANSWER: Because he has no sense of God's mercy to him. He cannot say, 'Great is thy mercy toward me: and thou hast delivered my soul from the lowest hell'; therefore he cannot say, 'I will praise thee, O Lord my God, with all my heart: and I will glorify thy name for evermore.'

But God has had great mercy on unawakened souls.

i. *He has had much sparing mercy.*

He has been long-suffering towards them. He has kept them alive many years, when they might have been in hell. He has kept the clouds of his wrath from bursting on them. He has kept back the Second Coming of Christ for them. But they have no sense of this mercy.

ii. *He has provided a Saviour for lost sinners.*

He offers Christ freely and fully to them as lost sinners, but they have no sense of this mercy. They have never closed with it. They are actually over hell; they are not delivered from it. They are out of Christ and heirs of wrath. The wrath of God is abiding on them. They cannot praise God. They cannot say, 'Thou hast delivered my soul from the lowest hell.'

Some of you are doubtless *unawakened*. You do not, you cannot, praise God heartily. You do not praise Him in your heart. You have no sweet thoughts of admiring love toward God. God is not in all your thoughts. You do not praise Him with your lips. You do not love to join in singing Psalms in the house of God. You never gather your relatives as a family to praise God every evening, morning, and returning evening. You never sing the praises of Christ in your sweet retirement, or, if you love the melody, you do not love the praise. Your thoughts are all about the tune and not about the words, as if you were admiring the golden censers of incense but cared not for the sweet perfumes that rise from within it. You never praise Christ in your life, you live to glorify yourself but never to glorify God.

How very plain that you never can dwell in heaven, for your heart is not turned to its Creator. If ever you would praise God in heaven, you must begin to praise Him on earth. If the lips are not opened in praises now, they will be sealed in eternal silence. They will be opened only to wailing and woe.

2. ANXIOUS SOULS DO NOT TRULY PRAISE GOD, NOR GLORIFY HIM.

It is not enough to be anxious about your soul. The anxious do not truly praise God.

i. *They do not praise Him in their heart.*

Their heart is much taken up with thoughts of God, but then they are all thoughts of dread and terror. They feel that God has been very merciful toward them, but this has excited their terror, not their praise, for they feel that they have always refused this mercy of God. They feel that there is a hell from which they must be saved, but yet they have not been persuaded to flee to Christ. They cannot say, 'Thou hast delivered my soul from the lowest hell.'

ii. *They do not praise God with their lips.*

They would fain sing praises, but they dare not. Being afflicted, they pray; but they are not merry, and therefore cannot sing Psalms. Praise can only come from a joyful heart. Now their heart is sad and weary. They may join in the melody, but their heart is not lifted up along with it.

iii. *They do not praise God in their lives.*

No doubt they put away all outward sins. An anxious soul dares not to go back to sin; but still they do not live a holy, thankful, eternal life, which alone gives glory to God.

QUESTION: Why is this?

ANSWER: Because they do not feel that they are saved yet. God has wakened them, but then they do not feel that they are brought to Christ, therefore they cannot praise. There is a great difference between being made anxious by God and being brought to Christ by God.

Many persons are made anxious who are never saved. Many persons are convinced of sin who are never convinced of righteousness. Many persons are made to beat on their breasts who are never made to praise God for redeeming them. Many were afraid of the flood who were drowned in it after all. It was only Noah and his family who were delivered and who could raise the voice of thanksgiving and praise.

And here I would speak to *anxious souls*.

i. *See here the time when you will praise God.*

Only when you have a sense of His great mercy toward you, and that He has saved your soul from the lowest hell. You never will and never can praise God heartily till then. You may try to praise before then, but your praises will be dull and joyless.

ii. *Do not rest till you can praise God.*

Remember you are not saved because you are all anxious. Many a sailor has been anxious in a shipwreck and drowned after all. His anxiety did not save him. The very devils tremble, but that does not save them. Anxiety is not salvation. Do not rest till you can praise God. Noah did not cease from his work till God shut him into the ark. Do not cease from your fear till God shut you into Christ.

QUESTION: May I not be a Christian, though I be not assured of my being in Christ.

ANSWER: Doubtless you may be a Christian without having any assurance of being safe. There are many trembling Christians who never in this life come to assurance of being safe. Yet still do not rest till you are sure of being safe, till you feel yourself in Christ, till you feel upon the Rock. You should not have a smile upon your face till there, and you cannot praise till then.

3. WHEN GOD BRINGS A MAN TO CHRIST, THEN HE BECOMES A PRAISING SOUL.

'I will praise thee.' When God brings a poor, weary, heavy-laden sinner to Christ then he finds rest, and when he finds rest then he begins to sing. There is no surer mark that a soul is brought to Christ than the opening of the lips in joyful praises. Thus the saying is fulfilled, 'Then shall . . . the tongue of the dumb sing' (Isa. 35:6). 'The tongue of the stammerers shall be ready to speak plainly' (Isa. 32:4). When the jailor was brought to Christ, then he rejoiced, believing, with all his house (Acts 16:34). His heart resounded with praises.

Just as when a bird has been snatched by the gentle hand of a deliverer from the cruel snare of the fowler, first it composes its ruffled feathers, and then, when in a sense of complete safety, fills the grove with its grateful melody: so does the soul that has been snatched like a bird from the snare of the fowler, when brought into peace and pardon and a sense of safety. Then that soul will lift aloud the voice of thanksgiving and praise. 'Though thou wast angry with me, thine anger is turned away, and thou comfortedst me' (Isa. 12:1).

A saved soul is even more a praising soul in that he has such humble thoughts of himself. He feels worthy of hell. And he has such a conviction of God's sovereign mercy, that God was not obliged to awaken him, neither obliged to bring him to Christ. And yet he has done both for him, a worm and a sinner. This it is which lifts up the heart to praise.

i. *He praises much in his heart.*

This is so wonderful an event that it is always uppermost in the heart. 'I love the Lord, because he hath heard my voice and my supplications' (*Psa.* 116:1).

ii. *He praises much with his lips.*

A true man of God, describing a time when many souls were converted among his people, says, 'Then was God served in our Psalmody, in some measure, in the beauty of holiness. Our congregation excelled all that ever I knew in the external part of the duty before, but now they sang with unusual elevation of heart and voice which made the duty pleasant indeed.'

iii. *He praises much in his life.*

He says, 'Thou hast delivered my soul from death . . . I will walk before the Lord in the land of the living' (*Psa.* 116:8–9). He feels bought with a price, and therefore glorifies God with his body and spirit, which are His. 'Come and hear, all ye that fear God, and I will declare what he hath done for my soul' (*Psa.* 66:16).

I would speak a word to *believers*.

Remember you are a people formed for God's praise. Is it true that you remember when you were the heir of hell, when, if you had died, you would have perished? And did God pour compassion on you and waken you to flee? When you sought after false Christs, did He hedge up your way with thorns and lead you to Christ? Has He done this with you and left others as you were? Has he thus dealt with you and will you not praise Him?

'Come and hear, all ye that fear God, and I will declare what he hath done for my soul.' Remember, dear friends, 'out of the abundance of the heart the mouth speaketh'. Commend the Saviour's love. Raise Christ higher every day in your thankful praises. 'The Lord hath done great things for us; whereof we are glad' (*Psa.* 126:3).

4. WHEN GOD BRINGS A SOUL TO HEAVEN, THEN THAT SOUL IS MOST OF ALL A PRAISING SOUL.

In heaven, these words have their completest fulfilment, 'I will praise thee . . . thou hast delivered my soul from the lowest hell.'

i. *Then the soul sees* FROM *what it has been saved.*

From the parable of the rich man and Lazarus (*Luke* 16:19–31), and from many other parts of the Bible, it would seem that hell is to be within sight of the redeemed in glory. They shall see that lowest hell from which they have been redeemed.

On earth we have poor and mean ideas of the dreadfulness of hell and the wrath of God. Even awakened, trembling sinners do not see one ten thousandth part of the dreadfulness of their situation. But in heaven we shall see it clearly. And oh, how loud shall our praises rise when we cry out, 'Great is thy mercy toward me: and thou hast delivered my soul from the lowest hell'!

When we see the pale, trembling faces of the Christless and see how they call on the rocks and mountains to fall on them. When we hear their cry, Who can abide these everlasting flames? Who can lie down in everlasting burnings? When we hear them wishing to die and not able to die, then we shall praise God far more loudly, far more heartily, saying, We were no better than they, yet thou hast redeemed us from the lowest hell.

ii. *Then, too, the soul feels TO what it has been saved.*

On earth we have poor and mean ideas of the blessedness of being saved. Even the most heavenly-minded believer has but a poor feeling of the value of salvation. But in glory we shall know far better the blessedness of being saved. Oh, that we guilty worms, worthy of the lowest hell, should be admitted into the highest heaven, that we who have naturally such wicked, hellish hearts should be made perfect in holiness, and in blessedness by God! And oh, to feel that we owe our all to God's free, sovereign love, to Christ's bloody death, to the Spirit's quickening grace! This will be heaven indeed.

Then we shall praise God as we ought, and far more than angels can. When we see God as He is; when we sit with Christ on His Throne; when the Spirit dwells in us for ever; then shall it not be the very heaven of heaven, to tell God that we owe it all to Him that we are saved by grace? When He crowns our brow with the crown of righteousness, shall we not cast that crown at His feet saying, 'Worthy is the Lamb that was slain.' 'I will praise thee . . . and I will glorify thy name for evermore. For great is thy mercy toward me: and thou hast delivered my soul from the lowest hell'?

Oh, believers, be much in praise, it is the mark of heaven. The strongest believers are strongest in praises. Spend much time in praises. Do not count it lost time. It is heaven upon earth. Praise him much in your hearts, and much with your lips, and much with your lives.

iii. *This is the very end for which God saved you.*

The candle is not lighted for its own sake. 'This people have I formed for myself; they shall shew forth my praise' (*Isa.* 43:21). 'Ye are a chosen generation . . . a peculiar people; that ye should shew forth the praises of him who hath called you out of darkness into his marvellous light' (*1 Pet.* 2:9).

You are of the same family as those in heaven. There is but one church and one family in heaven and in earth. We all should have one mark. Now in heaven they praise God. Do you do the same on earth?

But, oh, unbelieving souls! How plain that you shall never be in glory, for you do not love its occupations. Within the pearly gates of the New Jerusalem there is nothing but praise. Without are dogs. Be sure that if you do not love praise here, you will not love it hereafter. If you are not redeemed now, you will not sing the song of the redeemed then. All the learning in the world will not teach you that song, for no man can learn that song but they that are redeemed from among men (*Rev.* 14:3).

5

By the Rivers of Babylon

By the rivers of Babylon, there we sat down, yea, we wept, when we remembered Zion. We hanged our harps upon the willows in the midst thereof. For there they that carried us away captive required of us a song; and they that wasted us required of us mirth, saying, Sing us one of the songs of Zion. How shall we sing the LORD's song in a strange land? If I forget thee, O Jerusalem, let my right hand forget her cunning. If I do not remember thee, let my tongue cleave to the roof of my mouth; if I prefer not Jerusalem above my chief joy. Remember, O LORD, the children of Edom in the day of Jerusalem; who said, Rase it, rase it, even to the foundation thereof. O daughter of Babylon, who art to be destroyed; happy shall he be, that rewardeth thee as thou hast served us. Happy shall he be, that taketh and dasheth thy little ones against the stones (Psa. 137).

ISRAEL WAS A TYPICAL PEOPLE in every respect: in their bondage, in their deliverance, in their journey, in their food and water, in their falls and unbelief, in their victories, in their Jordan, in their rest in the promised land. They were a type of two things:

1. OF THE CHURCH OF GOD IN ALL AGES.

They are a company ransomed from bondage, carried through the Red Sea, fed by ordinances, a peculiar people, a people who shall together enter into a glorious rest.

2. OF AN INDIVIDUAL SOUL.

This is the best and clearest application of all. Even in their conduct in the Holy Land, in their not casting out all their enemies, they were typical of the Christian. Their captivities were typical:

i. of times when the church is persecuted, or torn, or afflicted by false teachers.

ii. of times when the Christian's way is hedged up, and he cannot see the face of his God.

Psalm 137 deals with Israel's captivity in Babylon. At such times as are typified there:

1. THERE IS A SORROWFUL REMEMBRANCE OF ZION.

'We sat . . . we wept . . . we remembered Zion' (verse 1). Zion is the place where God makes Himself known, His church. His presence in Zion brings joy. Where a true believer has fallen into sin, or into darkness, he sits down and weeps at the remembrance of his past joy.

You may remember Zion with tears. You may remember days when you were in Zion, perhaps in your youth – your first Sacrament; the influence of godly parents or godly ministers. You were then in Zion. You remember when the Sabbath was a happy day; but you have been taken into captivity and now you sit and weep.

If you really weep for the captivity you have come into, then be not downcast. This is a sign you are one of the real captives of Zion. Some of you are happy in sin. If so, then you never knew the Saviour. If you are mourning, then there is hope. 'Thou hast played the harlot with many lovers; yet return again to me, saith the LORD' (*Jer.* 3:1).

Do not sit and weep. Rather say with the Bride in the Song of Solomon, 'I will rise now, and go about the city in the streets, and in the broad ways I will seek him whom my soul loveth' (*Song of Sol.* 3:2). Those who seek shall find (*Matt.* 7:7).

2. THE WORLD DERIDES THE CHRISTIAN IN HIS ADVERSITY.

So it was with Israel. They were derided by their cruel spoilers who had carried them away from their home and their country and their Temple. When they saw them sitting down and weeping, they asked for one of their sacred melodies.

So it is with the world. They cannot always mock at the Christian. Oftentimes the Christian is filled with so strange a joy that they ask, What is this? Often the meek and quiet spirit disarms opposition, and the soft answer turns away wrath (*Prov.* 15:1). But when the Christian's day of darkness comes, when, through sin and unbelief, he has fallen into captivity, then does the proud world scoff and asks for mirth, Where are your psalms now, and your flights of joy? Sing us one of the songs of Zion!

Some of you may be feeling this just now. The face of your God is hidden, the beauty of Christ is absent, and worldly friends scoff at you, 'What is the good of being religious? This is how it will end! It will come to madness or melancholy. Sing now, if you can, one of the songs of Zion!' Remember, this is what Israel bore. Let your own wickedness correct you, and your backslidings reprove you (*Jer.* 2:19). Yet be not downcast. Even Christ bore such scorn, mockery and derision, as we see in Psalm 22 and in the Gospel records.

Some of you may be the cruel spoilers who mock at the weeping Christian. Take heed that ye offend not one of these little ones. He that toucheth them toucheth the apple of God's eye (*Zech.* 2:8).

Remember that awful sentence of God: 'Happy shall he be that rewardeth thee' (*Psa.* 137:8)! None ever mocked at the children of God and prospered. It was said of God's people: 'Blessed is he that blesseth thee, and cursed is he that curseth thee' (*Num.* 24:9). Those you mock may be in your own families. Fathers may mock at your children, brothers at sisters, sisters at brothers. Take heed and beware of this.

3. THE CHRISTIAN CANNOT SING IN CAPTIVITY.

So it was with Israel. They had their harps, but they hung them up in the willow trees. They said, 'How shall we sing the LORD's song in a strange land?' (*Psa.* 137:4).

So it is with the believer in darkness. He cannot sing. Every believer has a harp. Every heart that has been made new is turned into a harp of praise, till we come to the land where we shall get a blood-bought harp, a harp of pure gold. But whenever the believer is in darkness, his harp is on the willows.

a. *He has no sense of pardon.*

That which gives its sweetest tones to the song of the Christian is pardon. 'Though thou wast angry with me, thine anger is turned away, and thou comfortedst me' (*Isa.* 12:1). There is a peculiar melody in the song of a forgiven soul, but in darkness he cannot strike this tone. 'How can I sing the Lord's song in a strange land? How can I when I am on this dark mountain?'

b. *He has no sense of the presence of God.*

He is away from the Lord's house. That is the reason why Christians love the house of God: because He meets with them there. It is not the psalms, it is not the prayer, it is not the minister, it is not any of the creatures that makes the house of prayer sweet, it is the presence of the living God. See the whole of Psalm 42, and Psalm 84:10: 'I had rather be a doorkeeper in the house of my God, than to dwell in the tents of wickedness.' But when that felt presence of God is absent, then even the Lord's house becomes a howling wilderness.

c. *He has no view of Canaan.*

Its everlasting hills raise the heart to sweetest and loudest songs, but when he is in captivity that heavenly country is out of view. The waters of Babylon are proud but oh, they are not like the rivers of milk and honey! There is no scenery like the hills about Zion. The Christian in darkness cannot sing in a strange land.

Learn from this that it is an evil thing and bitter to forget Christ, to go into captivity. Are you able to sing your song? And do you have your harp always in tune? Oh, then, live by faith, keep close to Christ!

4. THE BELIEVER IN DARKNESS STILL REMEMBERS ZION

He prefers it to his chief joy. So it was with the Jews. A strange land was before them. A whole city with wonderful walls and hanging gardens and a thousand delights. But when they looked over all they said, 'If I forget thee, O Jerusalem, let my right hand forget her cunning' (*Psa.* 137:5)!

So it is with a believer in darkness. He often finds himself amid worldly pleasures and worldly friends when he is a captive in a strange land. Still he does not settle down among them, he looks over all and says, 'One day in thy courts is better than a thousand. If I forget thee . . . !' He cannot forget the joys of pardon and a new heart. The soul that has once tasted never can forget. It is the same with the bloodhound, that, when once it has tasted human blood, it never can forget it, and never will be satisfied with any other. Such is the Christian who has once tasted the grace which the blood of Christ brings. He never can forget it, never rest till he taste it again.

Some, I fear, are forgetting Jerusalem. You were once in Zion. You once counted the towers. But now you are forgetting. Oh, take heed, remember! Oh, do not forget! Some of you in youth promised fair, but oh, you have come into a dreary captivity. You have planted vines in a strange land.

Some of you never knew it. Babylon is your native land. You must seek the Lord, while He may be found.

Last of all, brethren, long for the heavenly Jerusalem, here we are but strangers and pilgrims. Oh, possess Jerusalem as your chief joy! Let the first of your desires be to be with Christ which is far better.

Do not forget the awful destruction of the enemies of Israel. So it was with Babylon. So it shall be with all that oppose the Israel of God.

6

Things That Must Be Done Now

Whatsoever thy hand findeth to do, do it with thy might; for there is no work, nor device, nor knowledge, nor wisdom, in the grave, whither thou goest (Eccles. 9:10).

MOST MEN IN CHRISTIAN LANDS lose their souls from not obeying this command. I believe most men have had their convictions of sin in childhood under the care of their mothers; or from their Sabbath school teacher; or at their first communion; or in serious illness; or at the first death in the family. Why did these impressions die away? Because they did not do what lay at hand, what their hand found to do. They put it off. Their goodness is 'as a morning cloud, and as the early dew it goeth away' (*Hos.* 6:4).

1. SOME THINGS DEMAND YOUR ATTENTION.

   i. THE CONVERSION OF YOUR SOUL.

You must not imagine that this is a work you are to do for yourself, or that ministers can do for you. It is a kingly work of the Lord Jesus. But it must be done. 'One thing is needful' (*Luke* 10:42). Other things you can do without. You can do without earthly friends, money, pleasures – but you cannot do without Christ.

'Except ye be converted, and become as little children, ye shall not enter into the kingdom of heaven' (*Matt.* 18:3). If ever you would know the peace, joy and holiness of God's children, you must be converted.

'Except ye repent, ye shall all likewise perish' (*Luke* 13:3, 5). If you do not obtain this, you will be cast away. All evil will come upon you. God himself will be your enemy.

ii. The Conversion of Your Friends.

Most of you have unconverted friends. Now, to seek their conversion is one of the things which your hand 'findeth to do'. When Rahab the harlot was saved, she also pleaded for her father, mother, brothers and sisters (*Josh.* 2:13). The rich man in hell wanted to warn his five brethren (*Luke* 16:27–31), and surely you have as great compassion as a soul in hell! You cannot bear to see them want temporal things, bread or clothing, how will you bear to see them cast away? They are put under your shadow.

iii. Your Sanctification.

'Follow peace with all men, and holiness, without which no man shall see the Lord' (*Heb.* 12:14). Every justified soul will be saved, but it will be in a way of holiness. The ransomed of the Lord return to Zion by the highway of holiness (*Isa.* 35:8–10). The righteousness of Christ is our whole title for heaven, but we must also have a meetness. The work of Christ for us makes us worthy of heaven. The work of the Spirit in us makes us ready for it. This one thing I do. This should be the chief business of life to work out your own salvation.

iv. The Advancement of Christ's Kingdom.

Every saved soul is a member of Christ's body. You now have no interest separate from Christ and his members. There is one body and one Spirit. If one member suffer, then all the members suffer with it, or if one member be honoured, all the rest rejoice with it (*1 Cor.* 12:26). Here every saved soul prays, 'Thy kingdom come.' A wound to Christ's honour is a wound to their peace. Their heart trembles for the ark of God. They love to help forward the work of the Lord. It is as it was in the building of the tabernacle. The nobles brought the precious stones, and the poor brought rams' skins and goats' hair.

2. HOW THESE THINGS SHOULD BE DONE – 'WITH THY MIGHT'.

i. We Must Use the Present Time.

Most men lose their souls and their advantages by procrastination. 'I made haste, and delayed not, to keep thy commandments' (*Psa.* 119:60).

a. *Is Your Soul Unsaved?*
Get it saved now! Now is God's time. Tomorrow is Satan's time. Youth is your best time, and every day you live it will be harder.

b. *Are Your Children Unsaved?*
Seek their salvation now! Begin today! Pray and use means with all your might. It becomes a harder work every day.

c. *You Need Holiness.*
Cast away your idols, now! Yield yourselves to God, now!

d. *You Are Called to Advance Christ's Kingdom.*
Do it now, and with all your might! Do not say, 'I will wait till the church is out of its troubles, I will wait till I see where our new churches will go.' Duties are ours; events are God's.

ii. We Must Break through Whatever Hinders.

When a man does a thing with all his might, he breaks through all opposition, as when a man runs with all his might, or cuts down a tree. So should we do in divine things.

a. *Seek Salvation Thus.*

There are many difficulties to break through. Perhaps you are involved in cares and worldly business, or surrounded with a circle of ungodly friends and companions, or your heart is attached and bound to some idol, or you see you will suffer loss or shame or reproach: still, do it with all thy might! Let all go! Break through all to come to Jesus. Jesus is worth a million friends and lovers.

b. *Seek the Salvation of Your Friends Thus.*

It is very hard to be surrounded with difficulties. Perhaps your friends despise you for all you say, or turn angry: still, do it with all thy might! Their reproaches will be easier borne now than when they come sounding from hell!

c. *Seek Your Sanctification Thus.*

Perhaps it will cost you dear. Some dear sin, some darling idol: still, seek it with all thy might, never mind what it costs.

d. *Seek Christ's Kingdom Thus.*

Again, there are many difficulties in the way. There are many adversaries, many to revile us. Still, go forward. Maintain ministers and missionaries, build churches and schools.

iii. We Must Persevere in It.

Be not weary in well doing. Seek salvation with perseverance. Some soon give over because they attain not. If you were to seek a thousand years and find Christ at last, it would be worth seeking. I would rather die, and drop into hell, seeking Christ, than draw back. God has nowhere fixed the time.

In seeking the salvation of others, love is long-suffering. Remember how long God waited for you.

In sanctification, be not discouraged by corruptions, fight on.

In advancing Christ's Kingdom, be not weary!

3. THERE ARE WEIGHTY REASONS.

i. THE TIME IS SHORT.

When a man has a long way to walk and little time, he walks fast, he puts out his strength. When farmers have much of their crop out, and the season is gone, they are in haste to get it in, they do it with their might. So should you! Your time is very short. The work very great!

ii. MOST OF YOU HAVE LOST YOUR BEST OPPORTUNITY.

Youth is the best time. Most of you have had the opportunity youth afforded.

iii. NOTHING CAN BE DONE IN THE GRAVE.

No one was ever made to repent or believe in Christ after death. There is no conversion below the ground. If you are not converted now, it will be never. No minister's voice will ever reach you then. You cannot seek the salvation of your kindred then. Soon you will be side by side in the cold grave, and you will not be able to utter a prayer for them or to speak a word of warning. You cannot put away your idols then. Your time is past. You cannot seek to advance God's kingdom then.

7

His Name Shall Be Called Wonderful

For unto us a child is born, unto us a son is given: and the government shall be upon his shoulder: and his name shall be called Wonderful, Counsellor, The mighty God, The everlasting Father, The Prince of Peace (Isa. 9:6).

THE PASSAGE BEFORE OUR TEXT is one of the most difficult in the whole Bible. Yet one thing is evident, that it is a message of light and joy and peace. In verse 2, the prophet refers to 'a great light' which shines on those who walk in darkness, and dwell in the land of the shadow of death. This light is like the rising of the sun. In verse 3, a joy is referred to which is compared to the joy of harvest. It is also likened to the joy of victory, as when, after a battle, men divide the spoil. How do this light and joy arise? Here is the answer: *For unto us a child is born . . .* (verse 6).

Ah, dear brethren, it is Christ given to the soul that causes all light and joy. It is this which gives light to the soul that is in the shadow of death. It is this which gives joy to the sinking heart, joy like harvest joy. Oh! that we may have the same light and the same joy in considering these words!

In the foregoing verses, the prophet clearly speaks of a wonderful change to be brought about in the hearts of his countrymen. They were in darkness but light is to arise upon them. They were in sorrow, but their joy was to be like the joy of harvest. They were under oppression, but their joy was to be like that of those who divide the spoil.

The wonderful change clearly relates to the One who is to come and to the revelation of His names. The doctrine we gather from this is: the names of Christ give joy and light to the believing soul.

Let us first, then, consider the names here given to Christ: 'Wonderful, Counsellor, the mighty God, the everlasting Father, the Prince of Peace'; and also the fact that the government is upon His shoulder. Lastly, let us briefly consider to whom this good news is addressed.

1. THE NAMES HERE GIVEN TO CHRIST.

Observe here that Christ has many names. Thieves and other evildoers are wont to take many names in order to conceal themselves, but Christ does so for the very opposite reason, to make Himself known. Every new name opens up to us something more of Him. His name is like ointment poured forth (*Song of Sol.* 1:3). Ointments were made up of several fragrant things. So Christ's Name is made up of many, which makes the fragrance all the sweeter.

It is like travelling in a hilly country: every few steps the prospect changes, although the place is still the same. Again, it is like a fine piece of music: many chords combine themselves to make the full melody. So the many names of Christ make full melody to the believer's ear. Or again, those are esteemed the best friends who are friends in many situations. Benefactors, visitors when sick, companions in health. So it is with Christ. He has many names because He fills so many offices.

Then also, a good physician has different medicines for different patients. So it is with Christ. To one He is the Wonderful, to another the Counsellor. On His head are many crowns. On His heart there are many names.

At the birth of a Prince it was customary that all his titles were given to him. So here, all these names are given to the little child who was to be born.

i. WONDERFUL

One divine, commenting on this text, says that Christ was made up of wonders. There was nothing in Him that was not wonderful. He is wonderful in His Person: God and man in one Person. He is wonderful in His love to sinners. He is wonderful in experience, when He reveals Himself to the soul. During His earthly ministry, all who came in contact with Him were amazed. 'Never man spake like this man', they exclaimed. He was wonderful in His miracles. All who saw them glorified God. And He is wonderful in every place: wonderful in the manger; in Gethsemane; on the cross.

a. *He is wonderful toward sinners.*

He is wonderful in His forebearance, in His seeking, in His freeness. When a soul is awakened, it is a cause of great wonder. David Brainerd's people were most deeply affected because Christ was so lovely, and yet their hearts would not close with so lovely a Saviour.

b. *He is wonderful toward His people.*

He is so in His rapid visits to their souls. Some have slidden back. Some have become unfruitful. Some have wickedly departed. Yet Christ is like a roe on the mountains (*Song of Sol.* 2:17). Whenever

His Name Shall Be Called Wonderful

your soul is aware, He reveals Himself (see *Song of Sol.* 6:12). He is wonderful in the way He clothes them. They are filthy beggars, but He puts on them his own robes of righteousness. He is wonderful in the way He carries them on His shoulder, in the way He restores them.

ii. Counsellor

He was the Counsellor in eternity, when He stood in the counsel of the Eternal Trinity. Looking down the ages to come, 'He saw that there was no man, and wondered that there was no inrercessor: therefore his arm brought salvation unto him' (*Isa.* 59:16). He took counsel with the Father and the blessed Spirit, and He said, 'Lo, I come . . . I delight to do thy will' (*Psa.* 40:7–8; *Heb.* 10:7). Then, also, He is the Adviser of sinners: 'I counsel thee to buy of me gold tried in the fire' (*Rev.* 3:18). And He is the Advocate of His people in the presence of the Father.

a. He is the Counsellor of Awakened Souls.

The Lord God has given Him the tongue of the learned (*Isa.* 50:4). God has put words like myrrh into his mouth for weary souls, like the dripping of honey. 'Come unto me . . . and rest.' 'I counsel thee to buy of me gold.' His name is Wisdom. 'Turn at my reproof.' I would say to awakened souls, Take not the world for thy counsellor. They say, 'Give up these gloomy ideas. Try gaiety, friends, books.' Remember Lot's wife. Lean not on man as counsellor. No minister! No book! Take Christ, for His name is *the Counsellor*.

b. He is the Counsellor of His People.

In Him are hid treasures, and all for your use. Everyone that has Christ has all that is in Him. A Christian is like a man who has goods in the bank, yet sits gnawing a crust by the wayside, or begging from passers-by. Go to your treasures and draw out of them. Some of you have greatly erred. Ah! You have forgotten the Counsellor.

iii. The Mighty God

This is a further source of great joy. The little child that was to be born is the Mighty God! Then He is a Surety of infinite value. His blood is the blood of the Mighty God (*Acts* 20:28)! His righteousness is the righteousness of God (*Rom.* 1:17).

Your sins may be infinite, but so is His atonement. If the Mighty God is my Surety, I cannot doubt for a moment that He is enough for me and His work sufficient to save me. I am complete in Him!

a. *This Ensures the Freeness of the Gospel.*

If an innocent man had died, it would have been sufficient for one guilty man. If an angel, perhaps for many guilty men. But if it was the Mighty God who died, then it is of infinite value. There is not a creature under heaven but we may go and say to him, 'The Mighty God is willing to be thy Surety, thy Covering!'

b. *This Ensures the Preservation of His People.*

He is able to hold me up. I am a stone, a clod. But if He be the Mighty God, He is able to hold me up. You may tell me of trials, temptations, devils, but if God be for me, who can be against me? (*Rom.* 8:31). In dying, I can confidently say, 'Lord Jesus, receive my spirit!' (*Acts* 7:59). 'The eternal God is thy refuge, and underneath are the everlasting arms' (*Deut.* 33:27).

iv. The Everlasting Father

It is by Christ and in Him that we are born again. Even ministers can say to those who are converted under their ministry, 'My little children.' They are born again by the word of God (*1 Pet.* 1:23).

Paul says, 'Though ye have ten thousand instructors in Christ, yet have ye not many fathers: for in Christ Jesus I have begotten you through the gospel (*1 Cor.* 4:15). But ministers are not the Father of our spirits, as God in Christ is. He will say of His people, 'Behold I and the children which God hath given me' (*Heb.* 2:13).

He will for ever protect and cover us as His children. An earthly father must sooner or later leave us orphans, however much he cares for us. But Christ has said, 'I will not leave you orphans' (*John* 14:18 [margin]). When He loves us, he loves us to the end.

And in eternity, He will be a Father to us. We shall follow the Lamb whithersoever He goes. He will feed us and lead us.

Oh! look to Him as your Father. In Him 'the fatherless findeth mercy' (*Hos.* 14:3). He counts us His children whom He has begotten again. He is our spiritual Father. He feeds us as His children. In Him we find a Father's love, a Father's care, a Father's faithfulness.

v. THE PRINCE OF PEACE

He reigns in the heart, and gives peace of heart, peace of conscience. He wipes out our sins with His bloody hand. Our sins, which are many, are forgiven us. He says, 'Neither do I condemn thee: go, and sin no more' (*John* 8:11). All the kings of the world could not give peace to an accusing conscience. Imagine a man, spiritually awakened, on his dying bed. The kings of the earth might compete to give him peace. One says, 'I will give thee half my kingdom'; another, 'Silver and gold'; another, 'A house full of pleasures'. Vain, all vain! As vain as the king who sought to make the sea retire from his throne.

But Jesus comes in, and reveals His wounds, and speaks peace, and there is peace! He is the Prince of Peace. Do you know this peace? Who can subdue the passions of the soul, or lull these fierce winds, these raging lusts, into rest? Jesus takes His golden sceptre and brings every thought into captivity. Oh! sweet and glorious Prince of Peace! By the Holy Ghost, the Comforter, He shall teach you all things. 'My peace I leave with you', He says. Our affections, thoughts, wishes, all fall sweetly under His sceptre. This only is repose, when we are in Jesus and Jesus is in us. Now look over all, and wonder, and adore. Jesus is all! May the Lord reveal Him unto you!

2. THE GOVERNMENT IS ON HIS SHOULDER.

Here we can but mention the comfort that springs from His being Head over His church, and Head over all things to His church. He who walks amid the seven golden candlesticks (*Rev.* 2:1) governs His church, and all things for the good of His church.

3. TO WHOM THESE GLAD TIDINGS ARE ADDRESSED.

They are addressed to us. At His birth, poor shepherds heard the angels say, 'Unto you is born . . . a Saviour, which is Christ the Lord' (*Luke* 2:11). Christ is to be exhibited to all the world.

He completed an infinitely glorious work of suffering and obedience, sufficient that all the world may come and find refuge.

Are all forgiven, then? No, by the dying of Christ, not one is forgiven. Elect and non-elect, all alike are standing without. God by free grace draws His own people to wash at the fountain. But all are bidden to wash, and it is as free to one as to another. Unto us is born a Saviour. But Christ is a Saviour in reality only to those to whom He is Governor, and all things else.

May God reveal Him unto us all. Amen.

8

God's Twofold Dealings with Natural Men[1]

Wherefore hear the word of the LORD, *ye scornful men, that rule this people which is in Jerusalem. Because ye have said, We have made a covenant with death, and with hell are we at agreement; when the overflowing scourge shall pass through, it shall not come unto us: for we have made lies our refuge, and under falsehood have we hid ourselves: Therefore thus saith the Lord* GOD, *Behold, I lay in Zion for a foundation a stone, a tried stone, a precious corner stone, a sure foundation: he that believeth shall not make haste. Judgment also will I lay to the line, and righteousness to the plummet: and the hail shall sweep away the refuge of lies, and the waters shall overflow the hiding place. And your covenant with death shall be disannulled, and your agreement with hell shall not stand; when the overflowing scourge shall pass through, then ye shall be trodden down by it* (Isa. 28:14–18).

THESE WORDS WERE FIRST SPOKEN to the men of Jerusalem, but they apply as fully to the men of our own town. There is perhaps no passage of the Bible which shows in such a remarkable manner the goodness and severity of God. Behold the severity and goodness of God; to them who refuse Christ, severity; but to thee, O believer, goodness, if thou continue in His goodness (see *Rom.* 11:22).

[1] Preached in St Peter's, Dundee, 1 December 1838.

1. THE CHARACTER OF NATURAL MEN

i. They Are Scornful.

'Hear the word of the LORD, ye scornful men' (verse 14). The same persons are spoken of in Proverbs, chapter 1: 'How long, ye simple ones, will ye love simplicity? and the scorners delight in their scorning' (*Prov.* 1:22). This is the character of almost all natural men.

a. *They Scorn the Wrath of God.*

They read in the Bible the plainest declarations of God's wrath against sin, and they feel in their conscience that they have sinned against God, and yet they refuse to tremble. They read in Romans 1, that the wrath of God is revealed from heaven against all ungodliness and unrighteousness of men who hold the truth in unrighteousness, and yet they refuse to flee from the wrath to come. When Lot spoke to his sons in law he seemed to them as one that mocked. When Noah the preacher of righteousness told the ungodly world of the coming flood, sinners stopped their ears and scorned his warnings. So is it still. The whole earth sitteth still and is at ease. They are not in trouble as other men. They are like wine settled on its lees.

b. *They Scorn the Mercy of God.*

They hear that there is a Lamb of God that taketh away the sins of the world, yet they do not choose Him as their Lamb. They hear that there is mercy for all who come, and yet they will not come. They hear that Christ is standing and knocking at their door, wishing to wash them in His own blood, and yet they will not let Him in.

Oh! are there none of you know what it is to be scornful men? You see others trembling for their souls, yet you never tremble. You see others feeling themselves lost who have done no more sin than you, yet you do not feel lost. You see others flying to Christ like a cloud, and like doves to their windows, yet you pass the Saviour by. You hear of others being converted to God, and yet you scorn the very name. You hate the very words, *conversion to God*. Ah! then you are the very souls here spoken to. Ye scornful men, hear ye the Word of the Lord.

ii. THEY HAVE REFUGES OF LIES.

I have often considered what was going on in the minds of natural men, when others are flying to Christ and they are keeping back. Now, here is their very heart laid bare by the heart-searching God: 'We have made a covenant with death.'

Some of you will think it impossible that you could be so impious, but just examine your heart and you will see that God is true, though every man should turn out a liar. Are there none of you putting off conversion to another day? You say, I am too young yet. I have seen too little of the world. I have not had my fill of its pleasures yet. Next year I shall begin to care for my soul. It will be time enough next year. Ah! This is making a covenant with death and an agreement with hell. You are acting as if you had bargained with death that he should not strike you till next year, and that hell should not receive you till then.

Some of you say you are too busy. Your business requires all your time. 'I have a family to support, and we must keep up appearances in the world, but when I have a more convenient season I will call for thee.' Ah! This making a covenant with death and an agreement with hell. How do you know that death may do his business before your business is done, and that hell may receive you before you receive a Saviour?

And then, you have refuges of lies. Every natural man is hiding beneath some refuge of lies. I shall mention a few.

a. *Ignorance of the Word of God.*

This blessed book is full of the clearest declarations of God's wrath against sin, all sin. It is full also of the plainest declarations of the true hiding place – the Lamb slain for sinners. But natural men keep themselves ignorant of what is in the Bible. They do not study this blessed book. They do not calmly search the Scriptures.

Oh! are there none of you proud natural men who leave the Bible unopened? Who never search it upon your knees? You think you will thus hide yourself from unpleasant truths. Alas! It is a refuge of lies, for the threatenings are there though you do not read them, and Christ is there, though you do not fly to Him. How soon will the hail sweep away this refuge of lies.

b. *'Perhaps the Bible May Not Be True.'*

'Perhaps there is no hell; perhaps there is no Christ; perhaps there is no God; perhaps there is no hereafter.' Are there none of you who cover your soul with a 'perhaps'? This also is a refuge of lies. For there is a hell. Whether you believe or not, yet he abideth faithful. And will you imperil your soul upon a 'maybe'?

c. *Amendment of Life.*

This is another refuge of lies. Some natural men like Herod hear ministers gladly and do many things. At such a time as this, when many are concerned about their souls, they become concerned also. They lay aside outward sins. They avoid the giddy world. They lay a bridle upon their raging lusts; they read the Bible; they begin to pray. Their friends and ministers begin to think well of them. They feel the change and begin to take peace in their amendment. Yet this also is a refuge of lies. Is there anyone hiding under his amendment of life? Oh! man, consider this, that nothing but a perfect covering can cover thee before a perfect God. Thine amendment is all imperfect. It is a refuge of lies. Whatever besides Christ gives peace to the soul before God, it is a refuge of lies. Christ is the refuge of truth, the true refuge. All others are a lie.

2. THE MERCY OF GOD TO NATURAL MEN

'Therefore thus saith the Lord God, Behold, I lay in Zion for a foundation a stone, a tried stone, a precious corner stone, a sure foundation: he that believeth shall not make haste' (*Isa.* 28:16).

Two things are to be observed here:

i. The reason of God's mercy;
ii. The matter of it.

i. The Reason.

Oh! what a depth of meaning there is in that little word, *Therefore*. Oh! what a window does it open into the heart of God. Oh! what a discovery does it make of the motives that lie at the bottom of the heart of God. Therefore, I say, 'O God, this is not the manner of men' (see *2 Sam.* 7:19). What would you have expected God to have said? 'Therefore I will cast you into hell, ye scornful men. Ye have scorned my grace and defied my power. Ye have made a covenant with death and an agreement with hell. You have made lies your refuge, and under falsehood have hid yourselves. Therefore behold, I cast you out of my sight into outer darkness.' Ah, no! God says, 'Therefore, behold, I lay a foundation stone.'

This is a great encouragement to scorners. Some of you feel that you have been scorners all your days. The law and the gospel have fallen upon your ears like an accustomed sound for many years. You have got into some secure refuge of lies where you can laugh at awakening sermons and bless yourself in your heart that you are not affected by them. And now, what do you think is God's mind toward you?

You think that he has no mercy for you. It is needless for you to turn, for He would not receive such an one. Ah yes, he would! You do not know God. He knows all your perversity, all your pride. He knows well every feeling in your proud, rebellious heart. He sees the frailty of the refuges of lies under which you are hiding. He sees that in a few short years the hail shall sweep them all away, and you will be left shelter-less, refuge-less, Saviour-less. God's eye pities you. God's heart spares you: 'Behold, sinner, just because you are so lost, I lay here a stone on which you may find rest.'

Oh, the mercy of God to sinners! It is like the great deep, it passes search, no human line can fathom it. Oh, sinners, how shall you escape if you neglect so great a salvation? How shall you escape if you turn away from him that speaketh from heaven?

ii. THE MATTER OF GOD'S MERCY.
a. *A Foundation Stone Laid by God.*
Now this is the very thing a sinner needs. By nature we all have houses on the sand. We may have been building all our life, but it has been on the sand. We have no place to stand on when the wrath of God shall come. The wrath of God is coming. It is an overflowing scourge. It is like Jordan which in Autumn overflows all its banks. It is like the Flood, when the fountains of the great deep were broken up and the tops of the highest mountains were covered. What will a sinner do in the swellings of Jordan? Where will you place your foot on that day?

Oh, sinner, you may scorn Christ just now, but you will change your mind in that day when it will be too late. See what God has laid as a foundation stone, the Stone of Israel, Immanuel, God with us, the Rock that is higher than we. 'This is the stone which was set at nought of you builders, which is become the head of the corner. Neither is there salvation in any other: for there is none other name under heaven given among men whereby we must be saved' (Acts 4:11–12).

Awakened sinner, if God laid Him, will you rest on Him? What will you place your foot on, if not on Jesus? You fear the wrath of God, but, behold, that very God has provided a hiding place. Oh! there is none of you too great a sinner, but you may rest on Him. There is none of you so small a sinner, but you must rest on Him.

b. *A Tried Stone.*

This Stone has been tried by God: God not only *laid* Him, but *tried* Him, tried if He were able to be a Saviour for sinners. Infinite wrath was laid on Him, yet he bore it all. Infinite obedience was required of Him, yet He gave it. And now God has taken Him up to his throne in token that He is well pleased. He is a tried Saviour.

It has been tried by man: Thousands have believed on Him and have found Him a sure stone for their soul to rest on. Never did any try Him and find Him an insecure Saviour. Thousands have tried Him in an hour of trouble when their sins came against them like a flood. They have found rest. None have been disappointed. Thousands have tried Him in an hour of darkness, when all their sins came over them like a flood. They have looked unto Him. They have cast their soul on this foundation and, in that valley, light has sprung up.

Oh, awakened souls, look round you! Many beside you have tried Him. Ask them if He failed them. Were they cast out? And why will you not try Him also? Though you had ten thousand souls, you might rest them all on that atoning Saviour!

c. *A Precious Corner Stone.*

He is precious in Himself, first, because he is Immanuel, God with us. If there is anything precious in the jewels and silver and gold of this world, it is all to be found in Christ as its Fountain, for He made them all. If there is anything precious in the unseen treasures of the heart of God, it is all to be found in Christ, for Christ is God. If there is anything precious in divine love, bursting forth from a divine bosom, even unto death, it is all in Christ, for He loved us and gave Himself for us.

He is precious in the eyes of the Father: When the Father chose a stone for sinners to rest on, He not only chose a mighty one, but one infinitely precious. Had He chosen the gems of the ocean or the gold of the mine; had He chosen one from among the glorious angels, it would have been precious, but oh! He chose the Jewel out of His own bosom, the gem of heaven's ocean! The equal of the Father! He is precious.

He is precious in the eyes of believers: To you that believe He is precious (1 Pet. 2:7). His blood is more precious than drops of liquid gold. His righteousness is whiter than any fuller on earth could white it. He is the Precious One. All things are to be counted but loss for the excellency of the knowledge of Christ. His atoning death is worth the agonies of a world of sinners. His perfect obedience is better than the obedience of a hundred angels. All other things fade when He approaches, like the stars before the sun. Have you seen Him? Have you known Him? Have you cleaved to Him? Will you ever part from Him? To you that believe, He is precious.

d. *A Sure Foundation.*

He that believeth on Him shall not make haste. When you place your foot upon a rocking stone, you are in haste to draw back your foot. Or when you are standing upon sinking sand, or on a shaking quagmire, you are in haste to find firm footing again. But Christ is a sure foundation. He that believeth shall not make haste. Awakened souls often hasten from one refuge to another. They go from mountain to hill, forgetting their resting place. First he tries one refuge and then another where he may rest his weary soul. But when he comes to Christ, he finds rest. He has no wish to change, no wish for another. 'Return unto thy rest, O my soul; for the LORD hath dealt bountifully with thee' (*Psa.* 116:7).

When others go away and walk no more with Jesus, he says, 'Lord to whom can I go? Thou hast the words of eternal life.' I have heard travellers tell of a serpent which has so bright and dazzling an eye that when a bird once catches sight of it, it is rivetted to the spot and cannot go away. But I know a wonder far greater than this: when once a fluttering sinner comes in sight of Christ, when once he has seen the atoning blood, the love and tenderness that are in the eye of Immanuel, he cannot withdraw. He is bound to that Saviour for ever. He that believeth shall not make haste.

Oh! You that have known Him, see that ye abide in Him. Keep Him and do not let Him go. Run your race with the eye upon Jesus. Pray with the eye upon Jesus. The more you are rivetted in His presence, the happier you will be. 'Their sorrows shall be multiplied that hasten after another god' (*Psa.* 16:4).

3. THE SEVERITY OF GOD TO SINNERS.

You have seen His mercy, now look for a moment at His strict and holy severity.

i. OBSERVE HIS STRICTNESS.

'Judgment also will I lay to the line.' This shows you the manner of God's procedure in judgment with natural men. You have seen a mason, when he is building a wall, apply the line and plummet to see if it is upright. He puts the line close to the wall and sees if the lead hangs evenly down. This is the very way in which God will judge all men. The holy law of God is His line and plummet. He will apply it to men's lives and hearts to see whether they are straight and upright. Oh! sinner, where will you appear? Your heart is like a crooked wall. Your life is like a tottering fence, and how will you stand in that day, when God judges you by line and plummet? Take the line and plummet of God's law and try yourself now and you will easily see that you are condemned. By the deeds of the law there shall no flesh living be justified, for by the law is the knowledge of sin. Oh! there is only one that can bear that the line and plummet should be applied to his righteous soul, the Righteous One. It is Jesus the sinner's Friend. He stood for sinners, and offers to be their refuge. Ah, sinner, be found in Him, and you will obtain mercy of the Lord in that day.

ii. Observe His Severity.

Oh, scornful men, if you will still scorn the Saviour; if you will still cleave to your refuges of lies; if you will still trust to your morality and being as good as other men; if you think still to stand before God, clothed in your own amendments; if you think to be saved at the last by a 'God help me' on your death-bed; or by a 'Lord have mercy on my soul' when you are plunging into eternity; if you will still neglect the great salvation, the Tried Stone, the Sure Foundation, then God has passed His Word, you shall feel the hail sweeping away your refuges of lies. You shall feel the waters soon overflowing your hiding place.

Be not mockers. Those who believe will not be ashamed nor confounded, world without end. Amen.

9

For the People Shall Dwell in Zion[1]

For the people shall dwell in Zion at Jerusalem: thou shalt weep no more: he will be very gracious unto thee at the voice of thy cry; when he shall hear it, he will answer thee. And though the Lord give you the bread of adversity, and the water of affliction, yet shall not thy teachers be removed into a corner any more, but thine eyes shall see thy teachers: And thine ears shall hear a word behind thee, saying, This is the way, walk ye in it, when ye turn to the right hand, and when ye turn to the left (Isa. 30:19–21).

IN THESE WORDS God describes the mercy yet in store for His ancient people, the outcasts of Israel. They have, for nearly eighteen hundred years, been like 'a beacon upon the top of a mountain, and as an ensign on an hill' (verse 17), but God is waiting that He may be gracious unto them. He is now waiting till the set time is come for having mercy upon Zion. When the fulness is come in, that is, when the full number are saved out of the Gentiles that are to be saved, then He will rise up and be gracious to His people.

---

[1] Preached in St Peter's, Dundee, December 1837.

When a soldier is in ambush, he lies still, he does not move; he waits till the set time be come, and then he rises up to the battle. So God has delivered 'the dearly beloved of His soul' into the hand of her enemies; He lies still, He does not move for them, He waits till the set time be come, and then He will rise, He will be exalted to have mercy on His ancient people. And what is it He will do for them?

'They shall dwell in Zion.' God will bring His ancient people out of all lands whither they have been scattered in the dark and cloudy day. 'I will plant them in this land assuredly with My whole heart and My whole soul' (*Jer.* 32:41). At Jerusalem they shall weep no more. Ransomed Israel shall be a happy people. They shall come to Zion with songs and everlasting joy upon their heads, and sorrow and sighing shall flee away. God will be the Hearer and Answerer of prayer unto them. At present God has 'covered Himself with a cloud so that their prayer does not pass through'; but when He brings them to Zion, Israel shall be a praying people, and He a prayer-hearing God.

Their teachers shall not be removed into corners any more, but their eyes shall behold their teachers. At present they have no true teachers. God hath given them the bread of adversity, and the water of affliction. The words of Amos are now fulfilled, 'I will send a famine in the land, not a famine of bread, nor a thirst for water, but of hearing the words of the LORD: and they shall wander from sea to sea, and from the north even to the east, they shall run to and fro to seek the word of the LORD, and shall not find it' (*Amos* 8:11–12). But when God brings back His people, He will raise up teachers, and their eyes shall behold their teachers.

The Holy Spirit shall be their guide. They shall hear a voice behind them. Their teachers are before their eyes, but a voice shall come behind them. The Great Spirit who teaches through the teachers shall guide them in the way of peace and holiness, saying, 'This is the way, walk ye in it, when ye turn to the right hand; or when ye turn to the left.'

Though these words do first of all refer to God's ancient people, yet, whatsoever things were written aforetime were written for our learning, that we, through patience and comfort of the Scriptures, might have hope. Learn then from these words the happy comfort of all true believers.

1. THEY SHALL DWELL IN ZION.

All unconverted persons dwell out of Zion. They are aliens from the commonwealth of Israel; strangers and foreigners. They are children of wrath. They have not the munition of rocks to defend them. They have not the favour and presence of God. They have none of the privileges of citizens of Zion. But when God brings a soul to Christ, that soul dwells in Zion. He is safe from wrath. As the mountains stand round about Jerusalem, so the Lord is round about that soul for ever. He is in the presence of God. He is brought nigh. God reveals Himself to that soul in another way than He does to the world. God is his Judge, his Lawgiver, his King, his Father, his God. He shall dwell there. God does not bring the soul once or twice into peace. The soul united to Christ *dwells* in Zion. He dwells in the secret place of the Most High, and abides under the shadow of the Almighty. Have you been united to Christ? Have you been converted? Then comfort one another with these words, 'The people shall dwell in Zion.'

They shall dwell in Zion above. It is a great joy to think that every soul that is united to Christ shall dwell eternally in Zion. I have no doubt there are some among you united to the Saviour. Well, here is a matter of joy. Every one of you shall dwell in Zion. Every one of them in Zion appeareth before God. Some of you have little faith, like a grain of mustard-seed; well, it shall grow, and you shall dwell in Zion. Some of you are in the wilderness; some in darkness, and seeing no light; some of you have fallen back into a cold formal state; still, I bless God, you shall dwell in Zion.

Some of you are not united to Christ. You shall never dwell in Zion; you shall never see the King in his beauty, nor the land that is very far off.

2. THEY SHALL WEEP NO MORE.

This also is true of a Christian. He weeps no more. When God awakens a soul that is lying in sin, that soul weeps bitterly. The beginning of a work of God is in tears. When there is a great outpouring of the Spirit upon any people, then there is, 'great mourning, as the mourning of Hadadrimmon', every family mourns apart.

In all times of revival it has been so; the land becomes a *Bochim*, a place of weeping. So when God begins a work of grace in any soul, that soul mourns, his closet becomes a Bochim, a place of weeping. Ah! this is little known in our day; and yet, wherever the Spirit of God is at work, He is sending some anxious souls away to weep alone. But when God brings the soul to Christ, that soul weeps no more. When the Comforter reveals Christ to the soul, a full, free, all-sufficient Saviour, he cannot shed another tear, unless they be tears of joy. He is comforted, he is calm, composed, at rest, he weeps no more. 'Return unto thy rest, O my soul!'

Have you been brought through this experience? Oh! see to it, my dear friends, now while it is called, Today, for you will weep eternally if you do not! Has this change passed upon you? If not, your case is inexpressibly sad!

Union to Christ dries up also all other tears. There are many afflictions to the righteous; still there is not one which union to Christ will not heal. This world is a vale of sorrow even to the righteous; a sinful heart, poverty, sickness, bereavement, and a thousand troubles without name often make the Christian weep bitterly. Still, in Christ he shall weep no more; in Zion there is a cure for every wound. If a man have pardon, and the favour of God shining on his head, and the Holy Spirit flowing into his heart, tell me what can harm him, what can be a real evil to him? Christ is a hiding-place from every wind. In so far as we are unbelieving, we may have many tears. 'I had fainted unless I had believed.' But if we abide in Christ, and the Comforter abide in us, what can hurt us, what can annoy? In Zion, thou shalt weep no more.

Christian, how little you dwell in Zion; how little of abiding in Christ there is; how little you dwell under the sheltering wings of the Almighty; no wonder there are so many weeping, dull, heartless Christians. Ah! if you would abide in Him, you would never be sorrowful, but always rejoicing. The tears of a Christian cannot be called tears; the tears of the world have the bitterness of hell in them; they work death; but your tears have the sweetness of heaven in them; you shall weep no more.

3. GOD WILL ANSWER PRAYER.

It is nowhere said that God is the Answerer of prayer to them that are out of Christ. He has nowhere covenanted to answer the prayers of Christless souls. He often does answer their prayers. You will find in Psalm 107, that 'they cry unto Him in their trouble, and He delivers them out of their distresses', but it is a peradventure. He hath nowhere bound Himself to hear and answer their prayers. Then you may say, 'If we be unconverted we should never pray.' Ah! if you be unconverted you should pray all the more, because your case is all the more sad and dismal, that God has nowhere bound Himself to hear your prayers; you should cry all the louder, 'O God, I beseech Thee, deliver my soul!' But when God brings a soul into Christ, He covenants to hear his prayer.

4. HE SHALL BE VERY GRACIOUS UNTO THEE.

Observe, He does not say He will do the very thing you ask of Him, but He says He will be very gracious unto thee. A child often asks his father for something that would be hurtful to him. His father says, 'No, my son, that would not be good for you. This is better.' He is very gracious to his child in withholding what he asks, and giving him something better. So it is with God. He often gives us more than we ask, and more than we think. Oh! what can I wish for more than that He should be very gracious unto my soul!

He will answer immediately. Some people say, God answers prayer in His own time. Some, that he treasures your prayers, and answers them all in a shower. But what does the Bible say? 'When He shall hear it, He will answer thee' (verse 19). Now, dear Christian friend, only believe, and it shall be done unto thee. All things are possible to him that believeth. If you will not believe, then you will receive nothing. It is easy to ask difficult questions about prayer and answers to prayers; but, oh! it is the hardest thing in the world to believe, to trust in Christ alone for righteousness, and to trust to God that He will answer immediately, just because he says He will.

5. GOD WILL PROVIDE TEACHERS.

Observe that when people are without ministers, God says they are 'eating the bread of adversity, and drinking the water of affliction'. How differently God judges from man! When a worldly man looks

For the People Shall Dwell in Zion

over our country, he sees the people all busy; plenty of work, and plenty of wages; plenty of bread for the poorest of the poor; he says, 'Oh! what a happy people. They are eating the bread of joy, and drinking the waters of gladness.' But what does God say? He says, 'There is a famine in the land. I have given them the bread of affliction, and waters of adversity.' And what does Christ say? 'I have compassion on them, for they are as sheep that have no shepherd.' Christians, be like God and Christ in this. Oh! do not say, 'There is plenty in the land', when there is such a famine of the Word of life. Do not say, 'We have got teachers ourselves, and we care not who may be without them.' If you be Christ's people, feel as Christ did.

God will provide teachers for his people. This is true in the case of individual souls. Whenever God begins a work of grace in any soul, He always provides teachers for that soul. Whenever God kindles a spark of grace, He always finds teachers to fan it. He will not quench the smoking flax. I remember a poor Christian confined to a miserable hovel. She could not go from home, and there was no minister to care for her soul. You would have said, 'God cannot fulfil His Word here.' But He did. In the wall opposite her window was an old carved stone, with these words for a motto, 'In Christ is strength.' At that window she stood, and fed upon the Word day after day. So God fulfilled His word, and her eyes beheld her teachers. Even although He should have to make the stones cry out, God will teach His people.

This is true also of a country. When God has a favour toward a country, He will provide spiritual teachers for them. It was so with Israel. For them He raised up his servants the prophets, rising early and sending them. It will be so again. When God brings back the captivity of His people, then He says, 'I will give you pastors according to mine heart, which shall feed you with knowledge and understanding' (*Jer.* 3:15).

And so it shall be with us, if only we be a people pleasant in the eyes of the Lord. God will raise up labourers for the mighty harvest. Our eyes shall behold our teachers. Learn from this where to look for more of the true ministers of Christ to our beloved land. We must look to God. 'Cursed be he that maketh flesh his arm.'

Steadily, firmly, and devotedly we must use all the means an all-wise God has put within our reach; but we must look above men, and even above kings, to the great King of kings. If we be His people He will provide us with spiritual teachers. If our ways please the Lord He will make even our enemies to be at peace with us.

6. GOD WILL ALSO GIVE HIS HOLY SPIRIT.

This is the greatest of all the privileges of a Christian. The Christless soul knows nothing of this. He has no voice behind him saying, 'This is the way!' The Christless have no guidance promised to them; they drift waywardly through the world. You have seen a log of wood upon the tide. It is carried hither and thither; it is moved by every wave; at one time it is cast upon the shore, again drawn back into the deep. So is it with an unconverted soul. He drifts along into an undone eternity. Again, you have seen a man travelling through a wood. He follows one path, then follows another. He is perplexed and lost; the farther he goes, he goes the deeper into the wood. He is all alone. He has no one to cry behind him, 'This is the way.' So is it with an unconverted soul. All like lost sheep have gone astray. They have none to guide, none to direct them. Are you Christless? Then this is your sad condition. But when a soul becomes united to Jesus, he receives the Spirit of Jesus, and hears a word behind him saying, 'This is the way, walk ye in it.'

The Spirit leads in the way of peace. And even when a soul has been brought to Christ, that soul still needs to be guided to Christ.

Oh! if you be Christians, still, you will know it the hardest thing in the world to be constant to Christ, to walk in Him, to trust to Him alone for righteousness. You may feel it easy enough just now to look to Jesus and have peace, but wait till an hour of temptation, when Satan brings your old sins against you. You will be tempted to flee to other ways for peace. How shall you be guided? In no other way than this, 'You shall hear a word behind you.'

The Spirit guides into the way of holiness. If you be a Christian at all, you will know how hard it is to walk in the way of holiness. The evil heart, the tempting world, and the devil himself, all try to beguile you from the paths of holiness. How shall you overcome? The Holy Spirit shall be as a word behind you, saying, 'This is the way, walk ye in it.' Some of you know what it is to be united to Christ. Seek to have the word behind you. Oh, seek it more and more! It seems to be but little known in our day.

10

The Day of the Great Slaughter[1]

And there shall be upon every high mountain, and upon every high hill, rivers and streams of waters in the day of the great slaughter, when the towers fall. Moreover the light of the moon shall be as the light of the sun, and the light of the sun shall be sevenfold, as the light of seven days, in the day that the Lord bindeth up the breach of his people, and healeth the stroke of their wound (Isa. 30:25–26).

IT IS WORTHY OF REMARK that, in all ages, the 'day of the great slaughter' has been the day of great blessing to the Lord's own people. God brings the light and the shade, in order that we may not have partial and contracted views of God's character.

1. When God poured down a Flood upon the world, that was a day of great slaughter. The towers fell, but it was also a day when God bound up the breach of His people. He carried them safely above the flood of waters, sailing in the Ark.

2. When God overthrew Pharaoh and his horsemen in the Red Sea, it was a day of great slaughter. They sank like lead, but it was a day also of deliverance to His people. They stood on the brink of the proud waters and sang to the Lord.

[1] Manuscript headed '30 April 1840. Thursday. For 7 June 1840'.

The Day of the Great Slaughter

3. So it will be at the last day, when God shall throw an ungodly world into hell. It will be a day of great slaughter, and all the towers shall fall. But it will be a day when He will bind up the breach of His people. He will say, 'Come ye blessed of my Father.' He shall wipe away all tears. They shall wave their palms and sing the song of Moses and the song of the Lamb.

As to the day here spoken of, it is called

1. THE DAY OF THE GREAT SLAUGHTER.

It is the day when all the enemies of Israel shall be slain: a great day which is coming. Leviathan shall be slain (*Isa.* 26:21 and 27:1). God shall come out of His place to destroy him. Gog the prince of Rosh, Meshech and Tubal shall be slain. They shall come against Israel like a storm. But they shall fall upon the mountains of Israel. God will come against him with pestilence and blood (*Ezek.* 38 and 39).

Antichrist shall be slain. That wicked one shall be consumed with the Spirit of Christ's mouth and destroyed with the brightness of His coming. 'She saith in her heart, I sit as a queen and am no widow and shall see no sorrow. Therefore shall her plagues come in one day. Death and mourning and famine and she shall be utterly burned with fire, for strong is the Lord God that judgeth her' (*Rev.* 18:7).

2. THE DAY WHEN THE TOWERS FALL.

There are many towers that will fall in that day. The day of the Lord shall be upon every high tower and upon every fenced wall and the Lord alone shall be exalted in that day (*Isa.* 11:12–17).

The towers of Popery shall fall in that day. They are lifting them up to heaven, but they shall be cast down to hell. The cathedrals, the monasteries, the mass houses, shall be brought low. They shall face their feared destruction like the walls of Jericho, and never rise any more. The cry will soon be heard, 'Babylon the great is fallen, is fallen, and is become the habitation of devils and the hold of every foul spirit, and a cage of every unclean and hateful bird' (*Rev.* 18:2).

The towers of Mahomet shall fall. The mosques and the minarets shall topple and rush down. The Mosque of Omar shall become like the dust of the threshing floor. The minarets of Mecca and Medina and Istanbul shall fall in one day.

The towers of paganism shall fall. The temples of Hinduism shall be swept away with that wind of destruction. The black temple of Juggernaut, stained with the blood of nations, shall be lain as the white leaves that are showered around it. It shall become as the sand on the shore of Orissa.

The promises to God's people in that day are very remarkable:

1. ABUNDANCE OF THE SPIRIT IN THE MOST UNLIKELY PLACES

'There shall be . . . rivers and streams of water.' It is possible that these words may be literally fulfilled. The mountains of Israel are parched for want of water. God has promised to Joel that all rivers of Beulah shall flow with water, but certainly the great meaning of the prophet is that there shall be abundance of the Spirit in the most unlikely places.

i. There Will Be Abundance, Rivers and Streams.

In dead times there does not fall a drop of the Spirit, the heavens are brass, the earth iron. Millions used to call this county, 'Poor, parched Angus.' Multitudes, multitudes in the valley of decision, but all dead. There are times when our parishes are like a great charnel house, full of dry bones. In better times, God sends a plentiful rain to confirm His heritage.

Drops fall from heaven. God plucks brands out of the fire. Such a time we have passed through. But in the time here spoken of, there will be 'rivers and streams', a flood upon the dry ground. A time of widespread awakening. A time when people shall be carried as by a stream of the Spirit toward Christ. And then it will be:

ii. IN THE MOST UNLIKELY PLACES.

It is not common for rivers to run down mountains. In ordinary times conversion is confined to ordinary places, to the families of the godly and church-going people. But when God pours out much of His Spirit, it comes to the most unlikely souls. The stream comes upon the hearts that are like desert mountains. It visits mills and factories, where the name of Jesus was all unknown. Heaven is taken by violence.

Pray for such a time. Ah! there are many of these unlikely places within the small compass of our own parish. Many high mountains and high hills, exalting themselves against God. I feel much that there are many families in this parish who soon will be in hell. Many that keep far away from the sound of the gospel and live in open sin; often meeting to sin, never to pray. Oh! pray for the time when there shall be rivers and streams. I fear much that there are many souls now hearing me, those of you that have passed through all the awakenings we have had, still unawakened. Those of you that are glued to the world, wedded to your old habits. Oh! pray for the day of great slaughter, when the towers shall fall. Pray for the rivers and streams.

Is there none of you who feels that you are one of the souls unlikely to be converted? Some of you feel that you are getting old, nearer the grave daily, with feelings that are getting blunt to divine things. You sometimes wish you had been converted, but you are not, and the uneasy feeling soon passes away while you sit in your easy chair and pass away your evenings in some pleasant game or an amusing tale. Ah! you are one of those who are unlikely ever to be saved. Oh, how you should pray that such a time should come.

Some of you may feel for your friends. You see them live on from day to day the same, dead in trespasses and sins, angry if you speak a word to them. Perhaps they will not come to hear the faithful preaching of God's Word. Pray for the time of rivers and streams.

2. SEVENFOLD LIGHT AND JOY TO THE LORD'S PEOPLE

When God sent the curse of darkness upon the land of Egypt, a darkness that could be felt, there was light in all the dwellings of Israel. So shall it be, in the day when the towers fall. Words can hardly be found more suitably expressive of the constancy and fulness of the light and peace of believers in that day.

i. THE CONSTANCY.

'The light of the moon shall be as the light of the sun.' Most believers in ordinary times have their seasons of darkness. In some they are almost periodical. Times when Christ is not plain to the soul. The way of Christ is dim and the conscience clouded, the heart filled with wandering mists. But in a time of reviving, these seasons of darkness pass away, the light of the moon becomes like the light of the sun. There is no night there.

ii. THE FULNESS OF LIGHT IN THAT DAY.

It is sevenfold what it is in ordinary times. At present, I fear, few believers come into the full light of God's countenance. The veil is

The Day of the Great Slaughter

rent, the way into the holiest is open, but few draw near to God. In times of reviving, when there are streams of the Spirit, Christ's people are brought into the palace of the king and say, 'Let him kiss me with the kisses of his mouth.' They are brought into the banqueting house and His banner over them is love. They are filled with all the fulness of God, like the widow who borrowed vessels from her neighbours and filled all with oil. 'Bring yet another vessel. There is not another vessel left.'

So full are the hearts of God's people. They swim in the love of God. Sin is plainly revealed in all its deformity, so that they hate it. Christ shines with sevenfold brightness on the soul; they are overpowered by His bright glorious beams. There is fulness of grace. God is known more, loved and adored.

Oh! how little of this have we now. Are you thirsting for this? Then pray for the day of the great slaughter. Some are afraid to pray for a day of slaughter. But observe, we pray for that day, not that we all may be spared, but that the Spirit may be largely poured out and Christ glorified.

God has bound up these two things together, so that you cannot long for the one without longing for the other. Many lose great peace and comfort by praying only for their private concerns. Many lose their life by seeking it. If you run after your shadow it will flee from you. Get a large heart. Pray for the honour of Christ. Pray, 'Hallowed be Thy Name', and so the time of light sevenfold will be hastened.

Be not discouraged at the clouds that threaten the Church of Scotland. It may be that an evil day is near, but I believe it will be short, and then will come the day of sevenfold light. And even in the hour of trouble, if you keep close, you may have much peace and inward light.

3. THE BINDING UP OF THE BREACH OF HIS PEOPLE

Israel has long been like a besieged city, Jerusalem trodden down of Gentiles; then he will bind up the breach. Israel has been like a wounded man whose whole head is sick. Then God will heal the stroke of their wound.

God's people are sorely divided. The body of Christ is almost rent asunder. In the day of streams and rivers, God will bind up this breach. There will be one Shepherd and one fold. As iron, when put into the furnace, all runs together, so the Lord's people, when visited with large measures of the Spirit, flow together. Pray for that time, the day of the great slaughter. Hate Popery with a perfect hatred. Never cease to pray that these towers may fall. Pray that the Spirit may be given like streams, 'Till we all come in the unity of the faith, and of the knowledge of the Son of God, unto a perfect man, unto the measure of the stature of the fulness of Christ' (*Eph.* 4:13).

11

The Silence of Christ[1]

He was oppressed, and he was afflicted, yet he opened not his mouth: he is brought as a lamb to the slaughter, and as a sheep before her shearers is dumb, so he openeth not his mouth (Isa. 53:7).

THE TRUTH THAT I WOULD BRING BEFORE YOU from this verse is that Christ was silent under His sufferings. I would show the fact that He was silent, both before man and before God – silent before Jews and Gentiles, silent before Pilate; silent in the Garden of Gethsemane, and on the cross. Then I would open up to you something of the reasons for His silence.

1. CHRIST WAS SILENT BEFORE GOD.

i. IN THE GARDEN.

The cup of God's wrath was set down before Him, the cup He was to drink. He might have said, 'This is none of mine; let them drink it that filled it.' But no, He only cries that it may pass. He acknowledges that it is just if the Father wills it. The second time He prays, He is satisfied of it and says, 'Thy will be done.' He acquiesces in the justice of God in giving Him such a cup to drink. He is like a lamb, He opens not His mouth to cry, 'Unjust!' His

---

[1] Preached at the sacrament of the Lord's Supper.

praying, 'Take away this cup,' shows that He did not deem it unjust. Prayer is the cry of one who feels he has no right to demand. If He had seen it to be unjust He would have demanded it; not 'Abba Father', but 'Righteous Father'. 'Shall not the Judge of all the earth do right?' (*Gen.* 18:25).

ii. ON THE CROSS.

Christ was silent as He hung in the darkness from the sixth till the ninth hour. Not once did He say, 'It is unjust; I am righteous and holy.' All the words of Christ on the cross are these:

a. When they crucified Him, 'Then said Jesus, Father forgive them; for they know not what they do' (*Luke* 23:34).

b. Later He said to the malefactor, 'Verily I say unto thee, Today shalt thou be with me in paradise' (*Luke* 23:43).

c. At the ninth hour, He said, 'Eloi, Eloi, lama sabachthani?' (*Mark* 15:34), not complaining that it was unjust, but rather showing the unspeakable dreadfulness of His agony.

d. He said to His mother concerning John, 'Woman, behold thy son!', and to John, 'Behold thy mother!' (*John* 19:26–27).

e. He said, in fulfilment of Scripture, 'I thirst' (*John* 19:28).

f. Again He cried, 'It is finished' (*John* 19:30).

These are all the words of Jesus on the cross. There was no rejection of His accusation. He was led as a lamb to the slaughter.

2. CHRIST WAS SILENT BEFORE MAN.

i. WHEN TAKEN.

A great multitude came with swords and staves and lanterns and torches. His servants began to fight, and said, 'Shall we smite with the sword?' Peter did. But Jesus forbade him. He was the Lamb. He could have called legions of angels to His aid. He could have taken away their breath; but He said, 'The cup which my Father hath given me, shall I not drink it?' (*John* 18:11).' 'This is your hour, and the power of darkness' (*Luke* 23:53).

ii. IN HIS TRIAL BEFORE CAIAPHAS.

a. When false witnesses accused Him, He answered nothing. 'He held his peace, and answered nothing' (*Mark* 15:61).

b. When the High priest said, 'He hath spoken blasphemy', and all answered, 'He is guilty of death'; when they spat on Him, struck Him with their fists, covered his face and smote Him with their palms; still He spoke not (*Matt.* 26:65–67). Every condemned criminal has a right to speak, and say why sentence should not be passed. He did not ask liberty. He was silent. Whenever He was asked if He was the Christ, or by Pilate if He were king, He answered readily; but when He was accused, not a word.

iii. IN HIS TRIAL BEFORE PILATE.

a. *The priests accused Him.* He answered to never a word, and Pilate marvelled (*Matt.* 27:14).

b. *Pilate sent Him to Herod.* He questioned Him in many words. The chief priests vehemently accused Him. He answered nothing (*Luke* 23:9).

c. *When Pilate gave sentence.* He had washed his hands; he could find nothing. Yet Jesus did not cry aloud, 'Unjust, unjust. I stand at Caesar's tribunal.' No, He was as a lamb, dumb.

iv. During His Mockery from the Soldiers.

They robed Him, gave Him a crown of thorns and a reed, bowed the knee, mocked Him as a king, spat on Him, smote Him. Still He spoke not. He did not say, 'I have never sinned.' He was as a lamb (*Mark* 15:16–20).

iv. On the Cross.

He gave no answer to men's taunts. Those that passed by, the priests, the thieves crucified with Him – all had their say, yet He opened not His mouth. They said He was an outcast from God. He felt it to be true, and He was silent (*Matt.* 27:39–43).

3. THE REASONS FOR HIS SILENCE.

i. All the Accusations Brought Were Just and True.

When a person is undergoing a trial, when he is accused, witnessed against, condemned and executed, if he be really guilty of the things laid to his charge, he is dumb, and says, I deserve it all. If he have any sense of justice left, he will be convinced and conscience stricken, and will answer not a word.

This was the very reason why Christ was silent. He had an infinite sense of justice, therefore He set his face like a flint in His taking accusations, condemnation, and execution. He felt it was quite just, therefore He answered not a word.

How? Had he committed the things laid to His charge?

No. He was God, infinitely holy. When He became man, He was called a 'holy thing' (*Luke* 1:35). He was always holy, harmless, undefiled. In death, He was a lamb without spot. But He came in the room and place of sinners. He was made sin for us, who knew no sin. He stood in the place of blasphemers, and gluttons and wine-bibbers, and deceivers and murderers and thieves, and outcasts from

God. These were all imputed to Him as much as if He had committed them all. Therefore, when He was accused, He felt it to be just and true. He opened not His mouth.

Oh, what joy this should bring to you that believe! Are you one with Christ? Then you shall never be condemned. 'There is therefore now no condemnation to them which are in Christ Jesus' (*Rom.* 8:1).

ii. HE WAS SILENT BECAUSE OF HIS COVENANT UNDERTAKINGS.

He felt Himself engaged to suffer all the reproaches that would be put on Him. The apostle could never have issued the challenge, 'Who shall lay anything to the charge of God's elect?' (*Rom.* 8:33), if all the charges had not been laid on the Substitute. Therefore I would say to the anxious, do not doubt whether you should take Christ as a Saviour. Do not doubt the truth of Him who was so faithful to His covenant, to His agreement with the Father. It was Christ's love to sinners that moved Him to undertake to suffer for them. Do you doubt His willingness to be your Saviour? See His love in these undertakings, and doubt no more!

iii. HE WAS SILENT BECAUSE OF HIS LOVE TO HIS SAINTS.

He was bearing the reproaches and accusations and wrath that were due to all those who would believe on Him. Had he stood upon his Godhead purity and refused to be accursed, had He refused the charges laid against Him, oh! then His people would have had to bear all the wrath due to their own sins.

iv. HE WAS SILENT BECAUSE HE SOUGHT HIS FATHER'S GLORY.

It was more glorifying to God that sin be punished in a divine Surety than in the worms that committed it. Therefore He delighted to do God's will. 'Lo, I come to do thy will, O God' (*Heb.* 10:9)!

All this is set forth in the Lord's Supper.

i. Why was bread chosen to show Christ's body broken for us? Its meanness showed the meanness to which He stooped.

ii. Then, it was broken bread, to show that He suffered death, and was broken in body and soul.

iii. The silent broken bread shows that He was dumb. He did not choose to represent Himself any nature that would complain or resist or cry. Bread resists not, it complains not. Just such was Christ under the wrath of His Father. This sets before us the plainest, simplest picture of the Saviour, broken in the room of sinners. It is a picture of the finished work so willingly undertaken by Christ, so thoroughly accomplished.

Some of you do not believe. Some do not consent that this silent Saviour has borne their sins, borne their wrath. Some will be asking the question, Did He bear *my* very sins. Some will not look to this Lamb of God. Ah! then do not be so inconsistent as to take the bread and wine.

Some believe. Then feed, appropriate Him, it matters not whether your sins are many or few. Say on taking the bread, 'As this bread was broken, so Christ was broken under the weight of the wrath that should have been upon me. He was silent under my accusations. He was broken under my wrath. He loved me and gave Himself for me.'

Christ was dumb because He would keep His word. I would say to the awakened, When you know that such a true Saviour has undertaken your cause, how can you doubt that He is enough for your soul?

12

Delighting in the Sabbath

If thou turn away thy foot from the sabbath, from doing thy pleasure on my holy day; and call the sabbath a delight, the holy of the LORD, honourable; and shalt honour him, not doing thine own ways, nor finding thine own pleasure, nor speaking thine own words: then shalt thou delight thyself in the LORD; and I will cause thee to ride upon the high places of the earth, and feed thee with the heritage of Jacob thy father: for the mouth of the LORD hath spoken it (Isa. 58:13–14).

THESE WORDS WERE ORIGINALLY ADDRESSED to God's ancient people, the Jews, scattered over every nation under heaven. Although the Sabbath was instituted at the beginning of the world, yet God gave His Sabbaths peculiarly to the Jews: 'Verily my sabbaths ye shall keep: for it is a sign between me and you throughout your generations; that ye may know that I am the LORD that doth sanctify you' (*Exod.* 31:13). But did Israel keep this sign of being God's people? Ah no! The Lord, by the prophet Ezekiel, says, 'My sabbaths they greatly polluted' (*Ezek.* 20:13). And did God bear with this awful provocation? No. It was for this that God carried them away captive, as it is said in 2 Chronicles 36:21, 'To fulfil the word of the LORD by the mouth of Jeremiah, until the land had enjoyed her sabbaths: for as long as she lay desolate she kept sabbath, to fulfil threescore and ten years.'

But will God leave Israel for ever scattered, and shall the land always enjoy its Sabbaths? Ah, no! The word of Ezekiel is yet to be fulfilled, 'I will take you from among the heathen, and gather you out of all countries, and will bring you into your own land' (*Ezek.* 36:24). Israel will be a changed people. They will no more pollute God's Sabbaths. They will keep their foot from the Sabbath and from doing their own pleasure. They will call it 'a delight, the holy of the LORD, honourable'. And then will God fulfil His promise. They shall call God *Ishi* [My Husband], not *Baali* [My Lord] (*Hos.* 2:16). They shall delight in the Lord, and God will make them ride triumphantly on their native mountains, and God will be a Shepherd to feed them.

The doctrine I would seek to demonstrate is this: Those who truly keep God's Sabbaths shall in no wise lose their reward.

1. WHAT IT IS TO KEEP THE SABBATH TRULY.

i. A RENEWED HEART KEEPS THE SABBATH OUTWARDLY.
This is shown in two ways:
By turning away his foot from the Sabbath.
By not doing his own pleasure on God's holy day.

a. *He turns away his foot from the Sabbath.*

You remember, when Moses turned aside to see the bush that burned, yet was not consumed, God called to him, 'Moses, Moses . . . Draw not nigh hither: put off thy shoes from off thy feet, for the place wherein thou standest is holy ground' (*Exod.* 3:4–5).

You remember, when the image of Dagon fell before the ark of God, that neither the priests of Dagon nor any of his worshippers would ever tread upon that spot where Dagon fell (*1 Sam.* 5:5).

You remember that the holy place in the temple was not to be trodden by any one but by the priests only. Hence the direction of the wise man, 'Keep thy foot when thou goest to the house of God' (*Eccles.* 5:1).

Just so, the Sabbath is a holy enclosure, marked out by God himself. It is called 'the sabbath of the LORD thy God', and again, 'The LORD blessed the sabbath day, and hallowed it' (*Exod.* 20:11). In the New Testament, it is called the Lord's Day. Every one that has a new heart regards the Sabbath as holy ground, as set apart from the dawn of day till midnight, entirely to God. He 'turns away his foot from the sabbath'.

b. *He turns from doing his pleasure on God's holy day.*

The expression, 'Turn away thy foot', seems to refer to outward travelling or business. This refers to pleasure. You remember when the money-changers and sellers of doves carried on their work in the temple – Christ regarded it as an awful profanation of His Father's house. But if people had gone for mere amusement, an excursion of pleasure, to admire the height of the walls, the size of the stones, and the gates of brass, I doubt not Christ would have regarded it as still greater profanation. 'My house shall be called the house of prayer; but ye have made it a den of thieves' (*Matt.* 21:13). So He would have said, Ye have made it a stage of gamblers, a place of merry-making. So with the Sabbath. If any one has come to Christ, he will not make it either a day of merchandise or a day of pleasure excursions.

Are there not many hearing me today who feel themselves condemned by this word of God. Are there none of you, my dear friends, who make the Sabbath day a day of merchandise? Are there not many who engage in baking or at least in preparing bread for the oven upon God's holy day? Are there not many who engage in the soul- and body-destroying occupation of selling spirits on God's holy day? Are there not some who make more money on the

Sabbath than on any other day? Are there not some who engage in their worldly business on the Sabbath evening? Ah, my dear friends, if I could speak with divine tenderness, I would do it, but I beseech of you, tonight upon your bended knees, to ask God if that is keeping your foot from God's holy Sabbath.

Again, are there not many of you who do your own pleasure on God's holy day? Are there not some who stay away from the morning service that you may sleep longer on the Sabbath morning? Are there not some who stay away from the afternoon service for the sake of a pleasure-walk into the country? Are there not many of you who spend the Sabbath evening in listening idly at your doors, in unholy company, in worldly conversation?

Dear Christians, it shall not be so among you – you whom God hath chosen out of this wicked place, perhaps the only ones that are to be saved in this place. Little flock, be ye *peculiar* in this. Keep God's Sabbath outwardly, the whole of it, every hour of it. Take the shoes of worldliness from off thy feet, for it is God's holy day.

i. A New Heart Keeps the Sabbath Inwardly.

This is shown in three things in particular:

a. *We are to call it a delight.*

It is an easy thing to keep the Sabbath outwardly, even with an old, wicked heart. There are many formalists who keep their foot from profaning the Sabbath, but they do not keep their heart from profaning it. They do not find their own pleasure, but neither do they find God's pleasure on His holy day. These have a name to live but they are dead. These are whited sepulchres, which outwardly appear beautiful to men but inwardly they are full of dead men's bones and all uncleanness. 'These are a smoke in my nose'

(*Isa.* 65:5). But to God's children, it is day of great delight. It is one of Christ's pleasant fruits. 'I sat down under his shadow with great delight, and his fruit was sweet to my taste.' To a new heart the Sabbath is the sweetest day of all the seven, for these reasons, among others:

1. *It is the day that Christ arose so early from the dead.*

The dawning of the Sabbath morning brings peace to every believing soul. So surely as the sun has risen on my dwelling this morning, so surely has God's face shone upon my soul, for this is the day my Surety rose from the grave. It is like seeing the place where the Lord lay. It fills the soul with inconceivable sweetness. Oh, believer! Is it not so? Christ is risen indeed. There is no day of the week when your soul is so cheerful. As Mary ran to bring the disciples word, so the soul runs and would fain carry the good news to every creature. As the disciples were glad when they saw the Lord, so believing soul, you are filled with gladness. Oh! Call it a delight!

2. *It is the day of double blessing.*

'God blessed the Sabbath day', and so, ever since, it has been a day of double blessing. 'In all places where I record my name I will come unto thee, and I will bless thee' (*Exod.* 20:24). So it is with all *times*. The Sabbath is peculiarly the time when God records His Name, and when He comes to us and blesses us. This is the day when Jesus first breathed on His disciples and said, Receive ye the Holy Ghost. The day when John was filled with the Spirit, 'I was in the Spirit on the Lord's day' (*Rev.* 1:10). And so it is still. It is the day when most have been converted and most have been comforted. Just as God said to Moses, 'I will meet with thee and commune with thee from above the mercy seat', so God says to Christians, 'I will meet with thee and commune with thee on the Sabbath.'

Oh! believers, is it not so? Is it not the jewel among the days of the week? Is it not the day when the shower comes in its season, yea, showers of blessing. Oh! Call it a delight. 'This is the day which the LORD hath made; we will rejoice and be glad in it' (*Psa.* 118:24).

b. *We are to call it honourable.*

When you really esteem any great man, you are not ashamed to declare your attachment and admiration before the world. If you really know Christ and love Him, you will never be ashamed of Him before men, and just so if you have got the new heart and really love the Sabbath you will not be ashamed to own your attachment before men.

Some are ashamed to show that they honour the Sabbath. When a party of friends is proposed for the Sabbath day, or an excursion of pleasure for the Sabbath evening, some are ashamed to draw back from it. They do not like it, they would rather not go, still they do not like to be singular. Ah! I fear you have not got the new heart, or you would call it honourable.

Again, when public profanation of the Sabbath is common, when great and rich people unite in openly pouring contempt on God's holy day, some are ashamed to lift up their faces against it. Some are ashamed to lift up their loud cry against the God-defying customs. Some are ashamed to be on the Lord's side. Some are ashamed to wash their hands of the Sabbath-breaker's guilt. Ah! see here, all who have the new heart should call it honourable.

Dear children of God, do not be afraid to be singular, you serve a singular God. You are a peculiar people, a peculiar treasure. Oh! be peculiar in this. Thou shalt not go with a multitude to do evil. Be not a partaker of other men's sins; keep thyself pure. 'Come out of her, my people, that ye be not partakers of her sins, and that ye receive not of her plagues' (*Rev.* 18:4).

I do think that the time is come to ask the question, 'Who is on the Lord's side?' I know you are but a little flock, and I know you have all the world against you, still the God of the Sabbath is for you. Oh! Call it honourable, dear Christians. In the face of newspapers, in the face of infidels, in the face of the world, let us hallow God's holy day and call it honourable.

c. *We are to honour God.*

Some persons ask, if Christians are not to do their ordinary business and not to do their own pleasure on the Sabbath, what are they to do?

The answer is: Thou shalt honour Him. It is the great day for honouring God. How is this to be done?

1. *By exalting Christ.*

Whenever Christ is exalted, God is honoured. Whenever Christ is despised, God is dishonoured. Only believers spend the Sabbath in exalting Christ in their own hearts, getting their hearts more and more rooted and built up in him. Be filled more and more with adoring thoughts of Him. Exalt Him before others, in your family. Especially do what Moses did, lift up the brazen serpent. So lift up Christ. It is the business of the eternal Sabbath. Let it be the great mark of your Sabbath: Glorify Christ!

2. *By meeting God.*

'I will meet with thee and commune with thee.' It is the great meeting-day of the soul with God. Oh! meet with God in secret prayer, in the family, in the house of prayer. Oh! When God comes down to meet with such hell-deserving worms, should we not spend all the day in meeting with God and communing with God? 'For a day in thy courts is better than a thousand. I had rather be a doorkeeper in the house of my God, than to dwell in the tents of wickedness' (*Psa.* 84:10). This will be the chief joy of heaven: we shall meet God. We shall know even as we are known.

3. *By praising God.*

'Whoso offereth praise glorifieth me' (*Psa.* 50:23). Praise is very much the work of the eternal Sabbath in heaven. It is of all things the most glorifying to God, because it gives God the glory of all His attributes and all His works. Praise, then, should be peculiarly the work of the Sabbath on earth. The happiest and most experienced Christians spend much of the Sabbath in praise.

Oh! are there some of you to whom the Sabbath is a weariness? 'When will the new moon be gone, that we may sell corn? and the sabbath, that we may set forth wheat?' (*Amos.* 8:5). Are there some of you who love the idleness of it, love to see and be seen, the walking out and the idle conversations. Ah! then you know not the joy of this holy day. It is no delight to you. Neither would heaven be if you were there. You would say, 'What a weariness it is!' Ah! how dreadful to have your very nature unfit for heaven, and fit only for hell.

3. THE REWARD.

This is both temporal and spiritual.

i. TEMPORAL.

There are some sins which God often visits with temporal judgments, and Sabbath-breaking is one of them. Those of you who notice these things will observe that the most dreadful accidents generally happen on the Sabbath. So God often rewards Sabbath-keeping by temporal blessings. It was a remarkable saying which Judge Hales left to his children, 'The observance of this day hath ever had joined to it a blessing on the rest of my time and the week that hath been so begun hath been blessed and prospered to me.'[1]

Let me exhort you to keep the Sabbath ever by this means: *consideration*. Consider, you that are not prospering in business, you who are cast down by unexpected losses and bereavements, whether Sabbath-breaking may not be at the root of it. Those of you who labour on God's holy day, see if God will not make your business prosper better by not doing so. He will be a Shepherd to you, and 'feed you with the heritage of Jacob thy father' (*Isa*. 58:14).

ii. SPIRITUAL.

This consists principally in delight in the Lord: 'Then shalt thou delight thyself in the LORD' (*Isa*. 58:14). We have spoken a little of this already, and the nature of it is best learned by blessed experience.

---

[1] Sir James Hales is mentioned in John Foxe's *Acts and Monuments* (*Book of Martyrs*) as a godly judge who 'showed himself to be a gospeller, no less by his word than deed, and no less at home than abroad'.

13

The Spirit of the Lord Is upon Me[1]

The spirit of the Lord GOD is upon me; because the LORD hath anointed me to preach good tidings unto the meek; he hath sent me to bind up the brokenhearted, to proclaim liberty to the captives, and the opening of the prison to them that are bound; to proclaim the acceptable year of the LORD, and the day of vengeance of our God; to comfort all that mourn (Isa. 61:1–2).

IT IS NOW TWELVE MONTHS since I first addressed you from these words. These twelve months have rolled over us. We shall meet them again in the Judgment. My object in choosing the same words today is that we may take one another to witness this day whether we have profited during the year that is past.

I wish to examine myself how far I have preached and laboured among you in the spirit of these words. I wish you to examine yourselves how far you have received that benefit under our ministry which it was intended by God to give. In climbing a hill it is pleasant to come to landing places, to look back how far we have climbed, to look up how far we have to climb. These words belong to Christ.

---

[1] Preached in St Peter's, Dundee, 26 November 1837.

The Spirit of the Lord Is upon Me

They were the first words from which He preached (*Luke* 4:16–32), and that was my reason for choosing them.

1. THESE WORDS SHOW THE OBJECT OF OUR MINISTRY.

The purpose of the ministry is to preach good tidings to distressed consciences, the meek and the broken-hearted. The *meek* here do not mean the gentle, or sweet-tempered, as the word is often applied to the children of God, but the afflicted, the poor – poor in their own eyes. Men naturally think themselves rich, that they have enough and abound. Here they are proud. They think much of themselves. But when God awakens them, they become poor, afflicted, without riches before God, naked, without a covering, without anything to recommend them to God. Do any of these things apply to you? Then you are here spoken of.

Christ was sent *to bind up the brokenhearted*. The broken-hearted are quite separated from their own righteousness. As long as a person has hope, their heart is whole. As long as a sailor's wife has hope that her husband's vessel may outride the storm, her heart is sound. Though she may have fear, yet she keeps up her spirits. But when the fatal news comes, when his loss is certain, then her heart dies. She sinks, she is broken-hearted.

So long as a person has hope of saving himself, of reforming, praying, weeping out his sins, so long he keeps his religion up. But when he is brought to see that he can do nothing to save himself, that it signifies just nothing, his heart dies within him. He sinks and is broken-hearted.

Now the object of our ministry has been first of all, with these distressed consciences. Blessed be God, there are some meek and broken-hearted souls in every place. I would desire to speak to such!

It has been our constant aim to speak to these whom God had wounded, the meek, the broken-hearted. This was Christ's way, this should be our way.

For a whole year we have told you the good tidings:

i. That Christ has died so that any sinner may take Him as a Substitute.

ii. That Christ especially offers Himself to the broken-hearted.

Oh! Why are you not brought to peace and joy in believing?

2. CHRIST CAME TO PROCLAIM LIBERTY TO THE CAPTIVES.

Who are the captives intended here? They are all men in their natural condition. They think themselves free, but they are the servants of sin.

i. SOME ARE CAPTIVES AND KNOW IT NOT.

Some follow daily after sin, yet they think they have complete liberty. Oh! this is one of the grand delusions of the devil.

ii. SOME ARE AWAKENED TO FEEL THEMSELVES CAPTIVES.

Those of whom I speak are in great misery because they feel their captivity. Christ came for such. He sends us to such. Our whole preaching is directed to such. I have sought to show you how you might be made partakers of the divine nature. Some are still in sin, its willing slaves. Some are still mourning, sinning and weeping, sinning and weeping. Oh! that you were wise! Is there no-one to whom the ministry has been blessed? Is there no-one who will cry, 'O LORD, truly I am thy servant; I am thy servant, and the son of thine handmaid: thou hast loosed my bonds' (*Psa.* 116:16)?

The Spirit of the Lord Is upon Me

3. CHRIST CAME TO BRING COMFORT TO MOURNERS IN ZION.

Those who 'mourn in Zion' (*Isa.* 61:3) are afflicted believers. To them, under outward troubles and inward, Christ sends us with a message of comfort. Troubles are both outward and inward. The outward troubles of believers are indeed many. Sickness and death come to all. I have been by the bed of death in many of your families; I have felt for your sickness, poverty and nameless troubles, and have pointed you to the only source of comfort. I have attempted to lead you to think as much of Christ and the glory that is to follow as of your situation, so that you have forgotten your troubles.

There are also inward troubles. It is possible for the child of God to walk in darkness and have no light (*Isa.* 50:10). Christ sends a message of comfort in the darkness.

4. CHRIST PROCLAIMED THE ACCEPTABLE YEAR OF THE LORD.

I have sought to preach to all, that the veil was rent and that every sinner might enter; that Christ was lifted up, and that every sinner might look to Him and live.

I would now appeal to careless, unawakened sinners. Have I not preached this? If I have, the question becomes, What use have you made of it?

5. CHRIST PREACHED THE DAY OF VENGEANCE.

This also is a part of the message of Christ, and always has been. And so I appeal to all who hear me, Have we not told you that if ye would not turn, then the acceptable year would become to you 'the day of vengeance of our God'?

14

The Harvest Is Past, the Summer Is Ended[1]

The harvest is past, the summer is ended, and we are not saved. For the hurt of the daughter of my people am I hurt; I am black; astonishment hath taken hold on me. Is there no balm in Gilead; is there no physician there? Why then is not the health of the daughter of my people recovered? (Jer. 8:20–22).

JEREMIAH has been well called, 'the weeping prophet', and indeed, of all the prophets whom God sent to Jerusalem he appears to have had most of the mind that was in Christ – the weeping Saviour. No prophet was more vilified and persecuted by his own countrymen than Jeremiah, and yet none poured forth from his bosom more of the tenderness and divine compassion which dwelt in the bosom of Jesus.

The more constantly they followed him with their threats and menaces, the more constantly did he follow them with entreaties and arguments. When they spoke against him, then he pleaded with them. When they persecuted them, then he pleaded with them and prayed for them. And when he saw that all his entreaties were vain,

---

[1] Preached as farewell sermon in Larbert and Dunipace; also in St Peter's, Dundee, 1837.

that the harvest was past and the summer ended and yet his people were not saved, when he saw how they despised the only Balm that is in Gilead and the Good Physician that is there, when he saw that all words were vain to persuade, then he wished for tears by which to persuade them. 'Oh that my head were waters and mine eyes a fountain of tears!' (9:1).

In the passage which I have read, there are two things which were obviously most prominent in the mind of Jeremiah and which were the causes of his plaintive cries.

1. That the best opportunities of being saved had passed by, and yet his people had not availed themselves of them. And,

2. That his people were about to perish, not because there was no Saviour, but because they would not come to Him to have life.

These were the two facts which were ever before the mind of the 'weeping prophet'. These two facts made him say, 'For the hurt of the daughter of my people am I hurt.' And these two facts made him wish for more tears than nature had given him, that he might weep day and night for the slain of the daughter of his people.

My friends, these two facts are as true of us as they were of Jerusalem, and it is my present object, by going over them in our own case, to stir up my own heart and the heart of all that are believers among you, to join with Jeremiah in his tears over perishing souls.

1. THE BEST OPPORTUNITIES FOR BEING SAVED WERE PAST.

'The harvest is passed, the summer is ended, and we are not saved.' Jeremiah seems always to have looked upon the sins of his people as a kind physician looks upon a grievous wound which is hastening the patient on to death. The false prophets around him were like false physicians. They healed the hurt of the daughter of his people slightly, saying, 'Peace, peace', when there was no peace. They only skinned over the wound without healing it underneath, so that it was sure to break out again with far greater violence than ever. But Jeremiah saw all the violence and venom of the wound, that 'the whole head is sick and the whole heart faint. From the sole of the foot even unto the head there is no soundness in it; but wounds, and bruises, and putrifying sores' (*Isa.* 1:5–6). He had come with healing messages from God, and yet all had been disregarded, his people were yet unhealed.

The warm season is well known to be the best season for the healing of wounds, and if the patient has let the year turn around without applying the needful remedies, it is to be feared he will not outlive the winter. Now this was just what Jeremiah saw his people had done. They had let all the best opportunities for applying the remedies and being healed go by without using them. 'The harvest is past, the summer is ended, and we are not saved.'

And now my friends, have we not the same cause for grief over the unconverted among you? How many among you are sick and perishing and yet have despised the only true remedy! You have had the best opportunities for conversion and yet have let them all go by. The harvest is past, the summer is ended, and you are not saved!

i. YOUTH IS THE BEST TIME TO BE CONVERTED, and yet how many have passed through their youth and are not yet saved.

a. The Bible says expressly, 'Remember now thy Creator in the days of thy youth, while the evil days come not nor the years draw nigh, when thou shalt say, I have no pleasure in them.' And again,

The Harvest Is Past, the Summer Is Ended

in Psalm 90, the prayer is, 'O satisfy us early with thy mercy; that we may rejoice and be glad all our days.' And again it says in Proverbs, 'They that seek me early shall find me.'

b. There is an obvious reason why it should be so. Youth is the season when all the passions spring suddenly into power. New and untried desires boil up within the youthful bosom, so suddenly that they boil over. There is a zest, a novelty, a tastiness in the pleasures of sin which urges on the youthful soul into all the excesses of sin, and then may conviction of sin be pressed upon the heart. Looking into the Bible mirror the soul starts to see his own image there. 'What!' he cries, 'Am I become such a monster as this? Have I slipped so easily into the very sins which once I was afraid to name?' And not only conviction of sin, but the gospel message comes with greater power. The heart is the tenderest in youth. The tears will flow even at a tale of fictitious distress. The heart is unenslaved by the cold and creeping selfishness of money-making manhood. Then is the time when the story of the Saviour's love cannot but come with freshest power: that He that dwelt in the bosom of the Father should have loved the guilty, the chiefest of sinners, should have died for His enemies, should seek those that do not seek Him and stretch out the hands after those that run from Him.

Ah! when God does bring this truth on a young heart, how it is overpowered. And when the old and hackneyed practitioners in evil, those who have sat unmoved beneath a thousand sermons, when they sit frigid and unawakened still, how often is the young heart breaking with the sense of sin and panting to embrace the Saviour!

But alas! how many of you have passed through that blessed season of youth and are yet unconverted? The harvest is passed, the summer is ended and you are not saved. You are like a sick man who has suffered the best season of the year to pass by without being healed, the warm season of the year is the best for recovery from sickness. And if the sick man let it pass over his head without regaining health, it is to be feared he will fall with the falling leaf and the snows of winter will whiten over his grave. Now this is just what you have done! You have let the season of youth go past you, and yet you are unsaved! You have passed through the time when your heart was most impressionable, it is most likely you will never be converted; it is most likely you will grow wickeder as you grow older, and as the hair whitens on your head, the frost will whiten over your heart.

Ah! then have we not cause this day to weep over you, yea, to wonder that we cannot weep? Awake then this day, I beseech you! And, like the traveller who should have been away by the dawn but has slept on till noon, and who rises to his feet and loses not a moment in hurrying away, to see if he can make up by present discipline for his past slothfulness, so, my dear friends, be awakened this day, by the very fact that your best opportunity is past! And, before another day passes over you, we may behold you a pardoned, happy child of God!

ii. WHEN THE HEART IS AWAKENED IS THE BEST TIME TO BE CONVERTED.

But too many have been awakened and let that time go by without being saved. There are few men pass through this world without a season of awakening. There are few men who go to their graves without having been at one time or another, anxious for their souls. God sometimes lays heavy sickness upon a man, leads him away from his merry companions and takes him by the hand to the brink of the grave and makes him look over into the eternal world; and when he comes back from the view he is an anxious man for a time. His face is like that of a man who has looked upon death.

The Harvest Is Past, the Summer Is Ended

Or God sometimes brings death into a blooming family and makes a break in the family circle round the hearth which never can be made up again. It is like the falling of a pleasant vessel, you may mend it but it will never be the same beautiful vessel again. God often puts anxiety for the soul into the hardest minds.

Or God sometimes brings anxiety for the soul into the unconverted bosom by infection from another. When a dear friend or neighbour is made anxious for his soul, and goes apart from our company, and prays with tears, and reads the Word with earnestness, the hardest soul is often melted by the sight. 'What!' he cries, 'Is my friend going to be saved and shall I stay behind to be lost? Is my dear friend going to join the peculiar people of God and shall I not cleave to the skirts of his garments?' In this way God brings many souls to cry out, 'What must I do to be saved?'

In these ways, and in many others, does God bring seasons of anxiety into many souls. Indeed I believe it may be fairly questioned if ever there was any soul that never had a season of anxiety for salvation. Ah! my friends, how many of you have had your seasons of awakening, either from heavy sickness or the death of friends or from seeing others converted?

You were made anxious for your soul. That season has passed away and yet you are not saved. Ah! if you knew the sadness of your own case you would cry out, 'The harvest is past, the summer is ended, and we are not saved.' You are just like the sick man over again. He is covered with wounds and bruises and putrefying sores which threaten death and yet he has let the very best season for healing go by and his wounds are only skinned over and not healed. So it is with you; from the sole of your foot to the crown of your head there is no soundness in you.

You were once made anxious about your soul. You once wept for your soul. You once beat upon your breast. You once read your Bible very earnestly. You once listened to the preached Word with all your heart, but that season of anxiety blew over, like the morning cloud and the early dew. Some worldly friend said, 'Peace, peace', when there was no peace, and so you live on, more and more worldly every day. You let the last time go by and are this day unconverted, you are not saved. Like Lot's wife you fled out of Sodom but, like her, you looked behind you and you are this day like a pillar of salt.

Awake then this day, I beseech you, and be like the farmer who has let all the best weather go past him without getting his harvest home, and who awakes at last to make the best of the broken weather that remains to him and to gather in by snatches his precious sheaves. So you, be convinced this day that you have let slip all the best opportunities for conversion already, that you have wronged your own soul every day that you have lived. And even amid the broken health and impaired memory of the downward years of life, may you be gathered into the presence of the Saviour.

iii. THIS DAY IS THE BEST TIME FOR BEING CONVERTED, and yet how many will let this day go by without being saved!

The whole Bible agrees in testifying that the present day is the very best day for being converted. From one end of the Bible to another, you will not find one word which would persuade you to put off one other day. It is always said, 'Now is the accepted time, now is the day of salvation.' This day are these words fulfilled in your ears, 'Today, if ye will hear his voice, harden not your hearts.'

It is the best because you may die before the next day. The ancients tell of a poor wretch who was condemned to sit down for a sumptuous feast with a naked sword suspended over his head by a single hair. Just such is the life of the unconverted in this world. The feast of sin may be rich and sumptuous and your appetite may be keen, but remember the sword of vengeance sways by a single hair. As long as you are out of Christ, the thread of life is all that keeps you from an eternal hell. And think for one moment who it is that keeps that thread from breaking, who is it that has kept you since you were born, through fevers and sicknesses and hair's-breadth accidents? Ah! it is the very Saviour Whom you are rejecting! By Him all things consist. Let Him but withdraw His hand and the silver cord would be loosed. The golden bowl would break, the pitcher would break at the fountain, and the wheel be broken at the cistern (see *Eccles.* 12:6). The body would return to the dust as it was, and the spirit, Ah! where would the spirit go? To the One who gave it. How can you then say, 'Today, or tomorrow'?

2. THE PEOPLE WERE ABOUT TO PERISH BECAUSE THEY WOULD NOT COME TO THE SAVIOUR.

If there had been no way in which Jerusalem might be saved, then Jeremiah would have been spared his tears. If God had brought no remedy into the world, or if that remedy had been beyond their reach, then it would have been hard to mourn, and Jeremiah would have sat him down upon the Mount of Olives like Jonah over against Nineveh, to watch and see what would become of the city.

He would not have shed a single tear. But when he knew that there was a balm in Gilead and that there was a Physician there, when he knew how often that Good Physician wished to have healed Jerusalem and she would not be healed, then it was that his heart bled for his infatuated countrymen and he wished for a constant supply of tears. He wondered that he could weep no more than he did. 'Oh that my head were waters.' And alas, my friends, have we not the same cause of grief over the unconverted among you?

When the angels kept not their first estate but left their own habitation, it pleased God to cast them down to hell and to reserve them for everlasting chains of darkness against the judgment of the Great Day. His eye did not pity, neither did He spare. God passed by these noble spirits; the Son of God, when he left the bosom of the Father, took not on Him the nature of angels, He did not die for them, He bore no curse for them, He was not offered to one of them to believe and be saved.

If, then, we were permitted to visit the realms of these fallen angels, if we could descend to the abodes of these spirits once so bright, so pure, so God-like, now so dark, so sinful, so devilish – if we could enter into their assembly and see their sad, wicked countenances, passed by, reserved for woe, we could not weep for them.

Our heart would fill with solemn awe, we would say, 'Our God is a just God and a Sovereign God.' We would cry out, 'Oh! the depths! Thy judgments are past finding out.' We would remember the word that is written, 'I will have mercy upon whom I will have mercy and I will have compassion on whom I will have compassion.' But we would not weep. We could not wish that our head were waters and our eyes a fountain of tears.

But, oh, my friends, how different a sight hath God put before our eyes! He hath sent us to fallen men, to those whom God so loved that He gave His only begotten Son for them, that whosoever believeth on Him might not perish. He hath sent us to you, to proclaim the acceptable year of the Lord, the year when you may ALL, ALL find peace and pardon through the blood of sprinkling. And the message which He hath whispered in our ear is, 'As I live, saith the Lord GOD, I have no pleasure in the death of the wicked; but that the wicked turn from his way and live: turn ye, turn ye from your evil ways; for why will ye die?' (*Ezek.* 33:11).

The Harvest Is Past, the Summer Is Ended

Ah! my friends, when that God who hath sent us to you and who cannot lie – when He hath said so plainly that He willeth all men to be saved and to come to the knowledge of the truth (*1 Tim.* 2:4); when He hath said again that He is not willing that any should perish but that all should come to repentance (*2 Pet.* 3:9); when there is such a balm in Gilead as the blood of Jesus; when there is such a blessed Physician there, how can we but weep in secret places for your pride? We must leave you as we found you, still unconverted, still hard-hearted and unbelieving. And will not every believing soul join with me this day in the heart-rending wish of Jeremiah, 'O that my head were waters!'

If there were no fountain opened up in the side of Emmanuel, where the guiltiest of you all might wash and be clean, then it would be vain to grieve for your perishing souls. If there were no rent veil in the rent flesh of the Redeemer, by which the vilest of you all might this day come in and have peace with God through our Lord Jesus Christ, then it would be vain in us to grieve because we left you under Jehovah's anger.

If the crucified Jesus were not a ladder set upon the earth whose top reaches into heaven, by means of which the meanest earthworm of you all might enter into the presence of God as boldly as the angels, it were vain indeed to grieve because we left you still crawling on this accursed earth.

If Christ were not a covert from the storm and the shadow of a great rock in this weary land; if He were not offered to the wickedest sinner of you all to shelter you from that wrath which is at your very door, then it would be vain and foolish to grieve because we leave you as poor, defenceless pilgrims in the waste, howling wilderness without a shelter from eternal woe.

If there were no balm in Gilead and no Physician there; if Christ were not anxious and able to pardon even those of you who have let the harvest go past and the summer come to an end without being saved, even those who have all along despised the Saviour and hated His messengers; if Christ were not this day with His whole heart desiring you to come to Him that your iniquities might be forgiven and your diseases healed, then we could leave you without one pang of regret, we would not even desire to shed one tear. We would say, 'God has passed these men by, and therefore we too should pass them by.'

But when there is a balm in Gilead and a Good Physician there; when Christ is a covert from the storm and the shadow of a great rock in this weary land; when the crucified Jesus is a ladder from earth to heaven; when there the veil has been rent from the top to the bottom; when there is a fountain in Jesus' blood to which the guiltiest may go; when there is a Saviour given as a ransom for all; when the Lord Jesus hath bid us this day declare that He does not wish the vilest, the sleepiest, the most vicious of you all to perish, Ah! how can we leave you thus unconverted, thus unawakened? How can we leave you just as we found you, not knowing that one soul has been wakened? That one soul has been redeemed from hell? That one soul has been brought to peace? That one soul has been edified? That one soul has been sanctified under our ministry?

How can we leave you thus and not cry to God to melt our own heart at least by the affecting sight? 'O that my head were waters, and mine eyes a fountain of tears, that I might weep day and night for the slain of the daughter of my people!' (*Jer.* 9:1).

15

Give Glory to the Lord[1]

Hear ye, and give ear; be not proud: for the LORD *hath spoken. Give glory to the* LORD *your God, before he cause darkness, and before your feet stumble upon the dark mountains, and, while ye look for light, he turn it into the shadow of death, and make it gross darkness. But if ye will not hear it, my soul shall weep in secret places for your pride; and mine eye shall weep sore, and run down with tears, because the* LORD's *flock is carried away captive* (Jer. 13:15–17).

THESE WORDS APPLY, first of all, to the Jews in the reign of Jehoiakim. Jeremiah had told them of their coming captivity and destruction by two singular images:

1. Under the image of a linen girdle carried away to the river Euphrates, and left to rot there, and

2. Under the image of bottles of wine, wherewith he would fill all the inhabitants of the land, and dash them one against another till they were destroyed.

---

[1] Preached in St Peter's, Dundee, 3 December 1837.

How did the Jews receive this prophecy? They received it with mockery and pride. They said, 'Do we not certainly know that every bottle shall be filled with wine?' And so they received it with pride, with haughty looks, they looked as if they did not care what God would do; as if to say, 'Let him do his worst, we care not.'

Then it was that Jeremiah began in a strain of the most touching eloquence to speak to his proud unbelieving countrymen, in verse 15, 'Hear ye, and give ear; be not proud: for the LORD hath spoken. Give glory to the LORD your God, before he cause darkness, and before your feet stumble upon the dark mountains, and, while ye look for light, he turn it into the shadow of death, and make it gross darkness. But if ye will not hear it, my soul shall weep in secret places for your pride; and mine eye shall weep sore, and run down with tears, because the LORD's flock is carried away captive.'

The doctrine I would gather is this: Unconverted persons should lay aside their pride and turn to the Saviour this day, lest they perish suddenly. I would show what it is to turn to the Saviour, why we should turn now, and that the children of God should weep, if unconverted persons will not turn.

1. WHAT IT IS TO TURN TO THE SAVIOUR.

This is described in two ways: not being proud; and giving glory to the Lord God.

i. CONFESSION OF SIN.

The first thing implied in these words is confession of sin, and lying down guilty before God. When Achan had sinned in taking the Babylonish garment and the wedge of gold, Joshua said to him, 'My son, give, I pray thee, glory to the LORD God of Israel, and make confession unto him; and tell me now what thou hast done'

Give Glory to the Lord

(*Josh.* 7:19). As long as a man hides his sin, from himself and from God, he is proud and robbing God of His glory.

a. *He is proud.*

He refuses to acknowledge himself a lost and helpless sinner. He says, 'I thank God I am not as other men are.' He refuses to lie down, at the mercy of a sovereign God.

b. *He is robbing God of His glory.*

Every man that is unconvinced of sin is robbing God of the glory of His omniscience. He says in his heart, 'The Lord doth not see. It was done in the dark. God would not notice it. It was done long ago. God will not remember it.' He is robbing Him of the glory of His justice. He says in his heart, 'The Lord will not avenge it. He will not write down such small sins in His book. Besides I have made amends long ago. I have mended my life and become a hearer in the House of God. God will not be severe upon us now.'

Some hearing me are in this condition. Some of you are proud, unhumbled, unconvinced of your lost condition.

1. *See how proud you are.*

You tread upon this earth as if it were all your own. You walk with a high look. You jest and talk and enjoy the pleasures of the world, as if all this were your birthright! Ah, woe is me! Pride was not made for man. You are a poor criminal under condemnation. Wrath is the only portion you can call your own.

2. *See how you rob God of His glory.*

You think Him just such an one as yourself. You make Him blind and weak and imperfect in His justice, as if He was an earthly king. Oh! If He would reveal Himself to you, you would see that you are immutably condemned. He was present at your darkest hours, yea, at the darkest wishes of your heart. You would see that He never can forget sin, for He is always the I Am, that He never can leave a sin unpunished, for He is infinitely just. I have often thought how a proud sinner will come in before God after death, naked, speechless, how he will lie down before Him. Oh! think of that now. You that are full of high looks, that think it beneath you to tremble at a sermon. Be not proud, but give glory to the Lord your God!

ii. Flying to Christ Is Implied in These Words.

As long as an awakened sinner refuses to fly to Christ, he is proud and robbing God of His glory.

a. *He is proud.*

It is pride more than anything that keeps men from flying to Christ. Often a man is made anxious about his soul. He is convinced of his lost condition and says, 'I must flee from the wrath to come.' But his heart is still proud. He thinks he can save himself. He hews out cisterns for himself. He compasses himself with sparks of his own kindling. He is going about to establish his own righteousness, and cannot submit to the righteousness of God.

b. *He is robbing God of His glory.*

Nothing is so glorifying to God as when a sinner flies to Jesus Christ. But if you will not come to Jesus you refuse to give God glory!

1. *You refuse God the glory of His love.*

He has loved sinners and provided His own Son to be a Saviour. You strip God of His glorious love. You refuse to give Him the glory.

2. *You refuse God the glory of His truth.*

He says plainly that Christ is free to the chief of sinners. You say, 'No, I dare not trust Him.' You make God to be a liar. You rob Him of the glory of His truth.

3. You rob God of the glory of His Justice.

If you would flee to Christ, then God's justice would be fully satisfied for all your sins. He will say, 'I am well pleased.' But if you will not flee to Christ, then you must suffer eternally, but God will never be satisfied, He will never say, 'It is enough!'

I would speak to awakened souls.

Are there any anxious souls, of whom Christ says, 'Ye will not come to me that ye might have life'? See here your true character: you are proud, and refuse to give glory to the Lord your God. You think it is humility, your keeping away from the Saviour. 'How dare I come to lay hold on such a Saviour? I am a depraved, polluted sinner.' Ah! this is the devil's humility. It is sheer pride. Oh, submit your judgment to God. Be not wiser than the Saviour. Be not proud, but give glory to the Lord your God.

2. WHY UNCONVERTED PERSONS SHOULD TURN THIS DAY.

Two reasons are given: the Lord has spoken, and death and judgment are at hand.

i. For the Lord Hath Spoken.

It is the Word of God, and not the word of man, that sinners must turn or die. I often find men living in sin who cannot be persuaded to flee from the wrath to come because they think it unmanly to flee at the word of a man, Shall I be anxious because of what a minister said? Shall I tremble at a sermon? Now here is the answer to that. 'Be not proud: for the LORD hath spoken.' It is the Word of the Lord, and not the word of man. It is God who says, 'The soul that sinneth, it shall die.' 'Cursed is every one that continueth not in all things written in the book of the law to do them.' My dear friends, despise our words as much as you will, call them contemptible, and treat them with contempt if you will. I care not. But oh, do not despise when your Maker speaks! Remember He is mightier than you. Remember you must die and be judged, and he that despiseth, despiseth not man but God.

ii. Death and Judgment Are at the Door.

'Give glory to the Lord your God, before he cause darkness . . .' Ah! This is a fearful picture of all that is coming on every unconverted soul.

a. *Before He cause darkness.*

The coming of death upon an unconverted person is like the darkness of evening coming on. Disease is often very slow and gradual, it creeps unnoticed over the whole frame, just like the twilight creeping over the sky. The old age of unconverted persons is often only gradual, like the coming on of evening. Faculty after faculty gives way, till their sun be really set. Oh! before the darkness sets in, I beseech you, awake and flee to the Saviour! Be not proud, but give glory to the Lord your God.

b. *Death is often very sudden and unexpected.*

The feet of the unconverted stumble upon the dark mountains. 'The way of the wicked is as darkness: they know not at what they stumble' (*Prov.* 4:19). The image here is taken from men travelling in a dark night. They walk on confidently in the dark, but suddenly they lose their way, and their feet stumble upon dark mountains. This is the way with all unconverted persons. They are walking in darkness. Suddenly death comes on them. To stumble upon a stone in the dark is bad enough, but to stumble upon dark mountains, this is terrible. Some unconverted people live quite secure all their life, but stumble at last on the dark mountains.

Give Glory to the Lord

They do not know where they are going.

Unconverted persons never inquire whether they are going to heaven or to hell. They go on confidently in the dark. They know not at what they shall stumble.

They take not the light of the Bible.

The Bible would be a light to their feet and a lamp to their path, but they do not love the Bible; there is no light in them.

They do not look to Christ.

Christ is the light of the world, willing to lighten every man that cometh into the world. But they will not follow Christ. They have no desires after Christ. Such are the unconverted. They walk in darkness.

What are the mountains on which they stumble? There are mountains of sins. The sins of a whole life-time are there. Before they appeared like molehills, but now they appear like mountains. There are mountains of wrath – dark mountains. Oh! it is a sad hour when the soul sees nothing but these dark mountains ready to fall on it.

I fear many hearing me are in a Christless condition. Oh! that I had Jeremiah's tongue and Jeremiah's tears, that I might warn you of these dark mountains. You think you will have some other time besides today to repent and turn. Oh, do not say so! Before this day is over you may be stumbling on the dark mountains. Oh, be not proud! Pride was not made for a poor sinner wandering on in the dark. Flee to Christ! Give glory to the Lord before your feet stumble on the dark mountains.

The hopes of the unconverted are all dashed on a deathbed. While they look for light, he turns it into the shadow of death. When a sinner is laid down on his death bed he looks for light.

He hopes to get better.

His case is very dark, and as gloomy as it may be. The physicians can give little hope and his friends look very dismal and sad; still he looks for light. He hopes that he will get better, that he will get the turn of the disease, and then all will be well. But when he looks for light, God often turns it into the shadow of death.

He hopes to be saved.

Few unconverted persons die without some hope of salvation. They look for light. 'I have not lived so wickedly as many of my neighbours', the dying sinner cries. 'I have been sorry for all my sins and made amends and now I look for light.' Oh! my friends the hope of the Christless shall perish. Many die full of hope and wake full of despair. When a Christless soul comes to the brink of an eternal world he stretches his eye to see if he can find any light but he finds only the blackness of darkness for ever.

I would speak to those without Christ.

I would persuade you by all the blessedness to be found in Christ, by all the misery of the outer darkness, to lay aside your pride and to give glory to the Lord your God. Deathbed after deathbed is coming on us; it may be your turn next. If you will join yourself to the Lord now, then surely the grave shall be to you the bed of graceful rest. You shall look for light and find an abundant entrance into glory. But oh! if you will not turn, your feet will soon stumble on the dark mountains. It is an awful thing to die Christless.

3. THE CHILDREN OF GOD SHOULD WEEP IF THE UNCONVERTED WILL NOT TURN.

'But if ye will not hear it, my soul shall weep in secret places for your pride; and mine eye shall weep sore' (verse 17).

Give Glory to the Lord

i. Let the Unconverted Learn Who Their Best Friends Are.

They are those that weep in secret places for your pride. You often think that your best friends are those who will eat and drink with you, and play games with you, and enjoy sin with you.

Ah, I will ask you one question, Do they care for your soul? Do they weep in secret places for your pride? No, they care not for their own soul, so how can they care for yours? But have you a friend that knows the Lord Jesus? Have you a child, a sister or brother, that knows the Lord? These are your truest friends. Although you do not like them, though you hate their ways, yet they weep in secret places for your pride.

Perhaps tears have been shed for some of you this day already. Ah, learn this, the Christians are your best friends!

ii. Let the Children of God Learn to Weep for Perishing Souls.

I fear there is little of this spirit among Christians now. I fear there are few among us who weep in secret places over the pride of unconverted souls. Cultivate this spirit, I beseech you!

a. *It will make you gentle and tender in your behaviour toward the world.* You will never rail at a man if you have been weeping in secret for his pride. It will keep you from being bitter against the world. Oh, how these tears would sweeten your spirit!

b. *Who knows how many souls would be saved if you would make serious use of daily weeping and praying before God*, over your unconverted friends and over the unconverted world.

Ah, did not David plead with his tears? 'Rivers of water run down mine eyes, because they keep not thy law' (*Psa.* 119:136). Did not Paul warn his Ephesians night and day, with tears (*Acts* 20:31)?

And did not the big round tear drop from the Saviour's eyes when he beheld Jerusalem (*Luke* 19:41)? He wept in secret places for her pride.

Dear Christians, be like David! Be like Paul! Be like Christ in this! I believe that God is setting a mark this day on the foreheads of the men that sigh and cry for the abominations done in the midst of us (*Ezek.* 9:4). May you be found in that blessed company and may your sorrow be turned into joy. Amen!

16

Can Thine Heart Endure?[1]

Can thine heart endure, or can thine hands be strong, in the days that I shall deal with thee? I the LORD have spoken it, and will do it (Ezek. 22:14).

EZEKIEL, WHEN YET A VERY YOUNG MAN, was carried captive by Nebuchadnezzar, king of Babylon. He was placed, along with a number of his countrymen, in settlements by the river of Chebar, a tributary of the Euphrates, two hundred miles north of Babylon. Here he prophesied for twenty-two years to his captive countrymen, whilst Jeremiah, his brother prophet, was similarly engaged in his homeland.

The prophecy before us is a prophecy against Jerusalem, 'the bloody city', and it was delivered, as we learn from Ezekiel 20:1, in the seventh year of his captivity, and about three years before the total destruction of Jerusalem by Nebuchadnezzar.

God had already begun his hard dealings with Jerusalem. He had 'hewed them by his prophets, and slain them by the words of his mouth' (*Hos.* 6:5). The king and many of the people He had sent into captivity, but all this was not enough; as the afflictions of

---

[1] Preached in St Peter's, Dundee, 18 December 1836.

Jerusalem increased, so did her wickedness increase. Sins before unheard of were committed in the midst of her, and God could stay His avenging hand no longer.

He was pressed under them as a cart is pressed under its sheaves (*Amos* 2:13) and now He would no longer delay the total destruction of the ungrateful city: 'Because ye are all become dross, behold, therefore, I will gather you into the midst of Jerusalem. As they gather silver, and brass, and iron, and lead, and tin, into the midst of the furnace, to blow the fire upon it, to melt it; so will I gather you in mine anger and in my fury, and I will leave you there and melt you. Yea, I will gather you, and blow upon you in the fire of my wrath, and ye shall be melted in the midst thereof' (*Ezek.* 22:19–21).

Such was the judgment that was at their very doors, but God does not afflict willingly nor grieve the children of men (*Lam.* 3:33). He has no pleasure in the death of the wicked (*Ezek.* 33:11). He would much rather overcome men by arguments than overwhelm them by His judgments. And therefore does He plead with Jerusalem in the words of my text: 'Can thine heart endure, or can thine hands be strong, in the days that I shall deal with thee?'

My friends, as long as you are out of Christ you are just in the very situation of Jerusalem. God is pressed under you as a cart is pressed under its sheaves. And though you may be very secure and hale-hearted, yet judgments are at your very door. Consuming providences are coming, and the death bed is coming, and the fearful plunge into eternity is coming, and the avenging Saviour is coming, His vesture dipped in blood (*Rev.* 19:13).

And just because God has no pleasure in your dying, but would rather you should turn, therefore has He sent us this day to plead with you before His judgments come, and to write the question of the text on your consciences.

Can Thine Heart Endure?

1. UNCONVERTED MEN WILL NOT BE ABLE TO BEAR GOD'S PROVIDENTIAL DEALINGS WITH THEM.

As long as God forbears to deal with unconverted men, they are contented and happy. A Christless soul is almost always in the days of prosperity a very secure soul. The chief reason is that God is not in all their thoughts, they do not feel that God is meddling with them. Their riches are daily multiplying. God seems to help their honest industry. Their health is vigorous and unimpaired. They know not what it is to be laid on a bed of sickness. Their friends are all around them, no chair is empty round the hearth and the joys of home are unbroken. They do not feel that they are in God's hand at all. They do not dream that they are under His curse. They cannot for a moment imagine that they are walking over the very pit of hell.

But when God gives wings to their riches and they flee away; when He casts them down with some sickness; when He breaks in upon the family circle and death is first known in the house, then they find out for the first time that there is a God, that He is meddling with them, that they are in His hand, that the Bible may be true, and the wages of sin may be death. Then is the time, when they see God's hand against them, then does their countenance change and their thoughts trouble them, the joints of their loins are loosed and their knees knock one against another.

Oh! my friends, think on the word: 'Can thine heart endure, or can thine hands be strong in the days that I shall deal with thee?'

Oh! infatuated men, you are now like the green bay tree and therefore you fear no evil. You are sound-hearted and strong-handed and you think it will be always thus, but remember it is written, 'If a man live many years, and rejoice in them all; yet let him remember the days of darkness; for they shall be many' (*Eccles.* 11:8).

Your neck is like an iron sinew – it cannot bend. Your brow is like brass – it cannot blush. But, oh! how you will be dashed in a day of adversity! How you will toss like a wild bull in the net, when your affairs are inextricably entangled. How you will rage and foam when all your money is gone. How your knees will become weak as water when your friends die and you hear God say, 'Write this man childless.'

You care not for peace with God and the indwelling Comforter and prayer and praise just now because you have got peace with the world and corn and wine and carnal joys. But the days of darkness are at hand, the cloud is already on the wind that is to darken thy dwelling. What will you do when all these earthly joys are poisoned to you? When you shall say, 'Call me not Naomi (pleasant), call me Mara (bitter): for the Almighty hath dealt very bitterly with me' (*Ruth* 1:20). You care not for the treasures that are in Christ: His fine gold; the riches of His inheritance in the saints, for you can cast your eye over your money-hills and you can calculate the coming interest and your heart whispers, 'Soul ... take thine ease' (*Luke* 12:19)!

But what will you do if these riches take to themselves wings and flee away? What will you do if thieves break through and steal them? God might make you a beggar this very night, and, oh! there is not a more desolate thing in the universe, than a Christless soul in adversity. Brethren, remember this word: 'Can thine heart endure, or can thine hands be strong, in the days that I shall deal with thee?'

2. UNCONVERTED MEN WILL NOT BE ABLE TO BEAR GOD'S DEALINGS WITH THEM ON A DEATH-BED.

In a former discourse, I attempted to show that the death-bed of the wicked is generally a very peaceful one. It is commonly thought that if men live very wickedly, they will die very awfully, that 'men may live fools, but fools they cannot die'. But this notion is contradicted, both by Scripture and by experience. The Bible plainly tells us, 'There are no bands in their death: but their strength is firm' (*Psa.* 73:4). And all who have watched by the death-bed of the wicked, can testify that they generally slip away without any disquietude, deceiving and being deceived.

Now though this is generally the case, yet it is not always so, and there are cases living on in the remembrance of most faithful ministers in which the unconverted have been unable to bear the dealings of God with them on a death-bed. It is more than flesh and blood can bear in that dreadful hour, and thus we have another meaning to the words, 'Can thine heart endure, or can thine hands be strong, in the days that I shall deal with thee?'

As long as the unconverted are in health and strength they live very secure lives in the world. Just as the giants before the Flood were not only mighty men in strength but mighty men in wickedness also; just as the children of Anak among the Canaanites were not only monsters in size but also monsters in sin; so is it very often with strong, sturdy, unconverted sinners, they glory in their strength and think they shall never fail.

Many things might awaken them to flee from the wrath to come:

Their long track of health and strength might itself awaken them. The goodness of God is intended to lead them to repentance.

A preached gospel might awaken them. It is continually sounding in their ears.

And the promise of the Saviour's Second Coming might waken them when 'the lofty looks of man shall be humbled, and the haughtiness of men shall be bowed down, and the LORD alone shall be exalted in that day' (*Isa.* 2:11).

The deaths of others around them might awaken them, when they see their comrades in sin, their boon companions, those that eat and drink and gambled with them, when these are cast down by their side without any work of forgiveness or of being new creatures.

All this might awaken them, but no, they live on unawakened, till their own turn comes. Stout in body and stout in sin, without Christ and without hope in the world, till they are smitten with incurable disease. Just as the highest towers fall with the loudest crash, and as the highest trees fall lowest in the storm, so these men fall from their height of strength and of security at once.

'Can thine heart endure, or can thine hands be strong, in the days that I shall deal with thee?' At first he thinks he shall recover, and his friends think so too. If the weather would improve, then he would improve, but he gets worse. His friends despair and now he must die. The minister tells him of a Saviour and a Saviour's love, but he has heard the very same a thousand times before. We tell him of the fulness, of the freeness, of the completeness of Christ, that there is no condemnation to them that are in Christ. But it is an accustomed tale.

Brethren, we cannot preach any other gospel to a dying man than that we preach to you. He says he is anxious to believe but he cannot. Faith is the gift of God and it is not given. Ah! who can tell what is going on within that racked bosom, tempest-tossed and not comforted. But you may read something in his quick eye, in his hurried looks, in his clenching hands that grasp at everything like a drowning man, eye hath not seen, ear hath not heard, the heart cannot conceive the things which God hath prepared for them that love Him not. Ah! brethren, you are strong and stout now, you can eat your meat with appetite and be merry in your sins now, but what will you do when going to meet your God?

3. UNCONVERTED MEN WILL NOT BE ABLE TO BEAR GOD'S DEALINGS WITH THEM AFTER DEATH.

Under the last head we have given a true picture of what sometimes happens, but oh, bear in mind that it is not generally the case. Men generally die as they have lived. They are generally stout of heart up to the dying hour, like some tall vessel gliding on with spreading sails before the wind. The sun shines brilliantly, the rippling waves smile round on every side. All is joy and mirth on board, but suddenly the vessel strikes on a hidden rock, and now to the coral rocks she is hurrying down, to sleep amid columns as bright as her own.

Like venturesome children upon new-made ice, they venture carelessly further and further. And though they may have some trembling now and then when the ice appears to crack under them, yet they persevere with all the daring glee of boyhood, till without a warning, the ice gives way and they are drowned in a moment.

Thus live and thus die so many unconverted men. They are set in slippery places. They are cast down into destruction. How are they brought into desolation as in a moment, they are utterly consumed with terrors. There are no bands in their death but their strength is firm. But what a change when they have taken the plunge into an unknown eternity! Just as it is true of the Christless, that their souls do immediately pass into perdition; just as Christ said to the dying thief, 'Today shalt thou be with me in paradise' (*Luke 23:43*), so does Satan say over every unbeliever's death-bed, 'Today shalt thou be with me in torments.'

You remember that no sooner had the breath left the body of the afflicted Lazarus than the angels bore him away in their happy arms to glory, and no sooner did the rich man die than he lifted up his eyes in hell, being in torments (*Luke 16:22–23*).

Ah! brethren, do you not see a new meaning to these words, 'Can thine heart endure, or can thine hands be strong, in the days that I shall deal with thee'? No unconverted soul has ever been able to bear it. No unconverted soul will ever be able to bear it.

i. *Now they shall believe in a hell.* Before they doubted if there were such a place. But now all of a sudden, they shall feel that it is true. Seeing is said to be believing. How much stronger proof, then, must feeling be? Before they could argue against it, they could quote texts against it, and grow very warm in argument against it. But now all argument fails, their wrath is stopped, they have not a word to say except to ask for a drop of water to cool the tongue.

ii. *Now they shall be disembodied.* Just as it seems necessary to the children of God that they be disembodied, because they could not bear in the body the glory of that light that shall burst upon them – our bodies are but cottages of clay and cannot endure much joy; these old bottles would burst if the new wine of the kingdom were poured into them – just so death is necessary to the children of wrath, that they may be able to bear the weight of their torments. The sudden plunge is more than flesh and blood can bear and therefore the spirit is unhoused and sent away alone to meet the fearfulness that shall surprise the hypocrites.

a. *If the body were there they might faint.* Sudden surprises do generally overcome the body and then they would be past feeling the pains of hell.

b. *If the body were there they might betake themselves to bodily comforts.* How often when a man is wretched on earth, he betakes himself to drinking or to opium to drive away his care, but there will be no drunkenness in hell, no opium in hell. There is no river of forgetfulness there.

c. *If the body were there, they might sleep.* Men on earth often sleep for sorrow and even pain sometimes lulls men to sleep. Some wretched men look upon sleep now as their chiefest enjoyment, and even there they hope to lay their wearied bodies down and sleep upon the tossing of the fiery waves. But there is no sleeping in hell. Even as it is said that in heaven they rest not day nor night, praising God, so it is said of the lost in hell that they have no rest day nor night, for the smoke of their torment ascends up before God for ever and for ever (*Rev.* 14:11). Their worm dieth not and their fire is not quenched.

d. *If the body were there, they might die.* Many a poor sinner here when he can find no rest anywhere else, seeks it in the grave. But in hell they cannot die, for it is written that they 'shall seek death, and shall not find it; and shall desire to die, and death shall flee from them' (*Rev.* 9:6).

Now, my friends, you may think it very wrong in us to speak to you so plainly about these things. Many were offended at Christ's words and walked no more with Him. And doubtless many of you will be offended if we speak as plainly to you as Christ did. But am I become your enemy because I tell you the truth? This is the truth that we have told you. As long as you are without Christ you may live calmly and you may die calmly, but all beyond is tossing and trouble for eternity. Oh! let not the infidel boast then that he can die as calmly as the Christian. Alas, your surprise will be all the greater, when like the rich man you lift up your eyes in hell, being in torments.

Oh, brethren, flee from the wrath to come! Remember you may be without any alarm just now, you may be quite at ease, whilst you are without Christ and without hope in the world. Remember too the question which God here puts to you. Think of it tonight when you lay your head on your pillow. 'Can thine heart endure, or can thine hands be strong, in the days that I shall deal with thee?'

4. UNCONVERTED MEN WILL NOT BE ABLE TO BEAR GOD'S DEALINGS WITH THEM IN THE JUDGMENT.

'Behold, he cometh with clouds; and every eye shall see him, and they also which pierced him: and all kindreds of the earth shall wail because of him' (*Rev.* 1:7). In a moment, in the twinkling of an eye, the trumpet shall sound (*1 Cor.* 15:52). The sound of that trumpet will be the sound of Jubilee in heaven. The happy souls in heaven may have listened to the sound of golden harps and the blood-bought harps of the redeemed for ages and ages, but the sound of the trumpet shall be sweeter than all, for it calls them to meet their glorified bodies, to be openly acquitted in judgment, and so to be for ever with the Lord. The souls in heaven are full of joy now, as full as they can hold. But then they know they shall be made capable of holding more, soul and body being filled to the brim with glory. The sound of that trumpet shall make all hell resound with wailing. The wretched souls that are there may have listened to the weeping and gnashing of teeth for ages of ages. But the sound of that trumpet shall be sadder than all.

Their heart shall die within them at the sound, for it calls them to meet their accursed bodies which they left to moulder in the grave, that body as well as soul may be tormented for ever. The souls in hell are full of misery just now, as full as they can hold. But then they know they shall be made capable of holding more misery, body and soul being filled to the brim with pain.

Oh! brethren, that day of the Lord is at hand. None of these Christless, poor souls shall yet be able to bear it. Who shall be able to stand, 'Can thine heart endure, or can thine hands be strong, in the days that I shall deal with thee?' 'And I saw the dead, small and great, stand before God; and the books were opened: and another book was opened, which is the book of life: and the dead were judged out of those things which were written in the books, according to their works' (*Rev.* 20:12).

Who can tell the joy of the believers when they are openly acquitted in the Judgment and go away into life eternal? And who can tell the misery of the Christless when they are openly condemned and depart into shame and everlasting contempt? Who can tell the misery of poor sinners in the hands of an angry God when they are to be cast into the lake of fire? Then the kings of the earth, the great men and the rich men and the captains of the mighty men and every bondman and every free man, in a word every Christless sinner shall hide themselves in the dens and in the rocks of the mountains and shall say to the mountains and rocks, 'Fall on us, and hide us from the face of him that sitteth on the throne, and from the wrath of the Lamb, for the great day of his wrath is come and who shall be able to stand?' (*Rev.* 6:15–17). Who shall be able to stand? 'Can thine heart endure, or can thine hands be strong, in the days that I shall deal with thee?'

Oh! brethren, whatever you be, if you be Christless, you will not be able to stand in that day. The greatest kings that have ruled over mighty nations, the mightiest captains that did not flinch from the very worst wars, that have been in battles and sieges; the sailors that have gone through the stormiest oceans and seen the waves running mountains high: none of them shall be able to stand. Their heart will die within them and their knees shall sink under them.

The stoutest hearted sinners, those that have been famous for laughing at religion, those that could swear and break the Sabbath without fear, they will be just as worms in the hands of an angry God. Ah! how will you be able to stand, poor feeble sinners, women, children, and you that are aged, tottering on the brink of eternity and yet out of Christ. Oh! how will you weather out that eternal storm. Oh! think now, think while it is time, think this night when you are upon your knees: 'Can thine heart endure, or can thine hands be strong, in the days that I shall deal with thee?'

17

The Way Hedged Up

Therefore, behold, I will hedge up thy way with thorns, and make a wall, that she shall not find her paths (Hos. 2:6).

THIS PASSAGE IN THE PROPHECY OF HOSEA speaks of God's dealings with backsliding Israel. They had gone away from God to idols, yet God was resolved not to cast away His people. He says that He will hedge up their way with thorns and a wall, so that they may seek their false gods in vain, and that they may return to the true God. Thus God often deals with sinners, and also with backslidden Christians.

1. GOD USES DISTRESS TO HEDGE UP THE WAY OF SINNERS.

It is frequently with the thorns of distresses that God hedges up the way, so that the sinner may return to Jesus Christ.

In time of health, natural men add sin to sin. God often sends sore sickness. Sometimes they run upon thorns, or a wall appears to hinder their further progress. The heart would fain press on, but it cannot. Then does God sometimes allure the heart to say, 'I will go and return to my first husband' (*Hos.* 2:7).

I would apply the truth of this to different classes of hearers:

i. To Sinners in Time of Health and Prosperity.

To these I would say, Pray God to hedge up your way, to hinder your further progress in sin.

ii. To Backsliders in Time of Health and Prosperity.

To you also I would say, Pray God to hedge up your way, and in this manner to do for you what you cannot do for yourselves.

iii. To Those under Distress.

It is God who is hedging up your way. It is God who put the thorns there. Be sure that you say, 'I will go and return to my first husband; for then was it better with me than now' (verse 7).

And I would urge this in particular on backsliders under distress. In faithfulness God is afflicting you, to bring you back to Himself.

2. GOD OFTEN HEDGES UP THE WAY OF BACKSLIDERS.

It is observable that God often hedges up the way of self-righteousness with thorns, and makes a wall in the path of the backslider, to draw the soul to Jesus Christ, her only true Husband.

i. To Christians Who Have Backslidden.

Souls once joined to Christ think that they shall never stray. But alas! it is sadly possible. Israel, as we see here, was typical of such. She said, 'I will go after my lovers, that give me my bread and my water, my wool and my flax, mine oil and my drink' (verse 5). See here how she is beguiled. It is for bread, water and the rest.

a. It is always the show of something good that beguiles the Christian.

b. It is often the seeking of worldly goods, riches, and comforts.

c. The backsliding Christian is deceived. 'She did not know that I gave her' all these things (verse 8). If you would only abide in Christ, you would have all things added unto you.

And so I would say to Christians: In Christ 'all things are yours' (*1 Cor.* 3:21). You will not be a loser by your religion. God has the corn, wine, oil, silver and gold to give and, if they are good for you, He will give them. Fear not!

And to backsliders I would say: You are deceived if you think to make yourself rich by forsaking God and Christ. 'Seek ye first the kingdom of God, and his righteousness; and all these things shall be added unto you' (*Matt.* 6:34). He gives the corn and the oil and the wine. Abide in Him, and you will not lack any good thing.

ii. GOD'S DEALINGS WITH BACKSLIDERS.

'I will hedge up thy way with thorns, and make a wall.' When a Christian is running away from Christ, going back to worldliness and sin, God sometimes suffers the path to be smooth for a little. The believer thinks he is going to reconcile God and mammon. He will spend a time with both, his first lovers and Christ; but soon the faithful God puts a hedge of thorns in his way. He runs upon the thorns, and stands bleeding and dejected.

But perhaps he may struggle through the hedge. Then God puts down a stone wall, over which he cannot climb.

a. *See here the faithfulness of God.*

'Thou in faithfulness hast afflicted me' (*Psa.* 119:75). If God were to deal with the sinner as he deserves, He would let him go; but God remembers His covenant and He uses the rod and stripes.

b. *See here the meaning of your afflictions.*

Christians, has God sent some pain and trouble, thorns in your path? These are God's hedges, to keep you from running after your lovers. Or perhaps you have struggled through the hedge, but now there is a stone wall. God has taken away all possibility of your going after your lovers. Bless God for these afflictions!

Backsliders, see here that God *must* afflict you. If you are bound in the bonds of the covenant of grace, God in faithfulness *must* afflict you. 'Bonds and afflictions abide you', if you are departing from Christ. You will run upon the hedge and the wall. Turn you, turn you, 'why should ye be stricken any more?' (*Isa.* 1:5).

iii. The Backslider's Determination.

'I will go and return to my first husband' (*Hos.* 2:7).

Oh, happy determination! Jesus is the first husband of the believing soul, and when he runs into the thorns, the believer says, 'I will return.'

The reason is also given in this verse: 'For then was it better with me than now'. How much better are joy and peace in believing than a hedge of thorns, with an uneasy conscience.

I would seek to persuade backsliders to return to Jesus Christ. Some are for staying where they are, among the thorns. Some need to be stricken again and again. Oh! learn the lesson soon. Remember the day of your espousal, your time of gladness, your song of praise. Return, ye backsliding children. If you be in the covenant God must repeat His afflictions, His hedges, His wall till you return. Oh, then, return!

18

O Israel, Return!

O Israel, return unto the LORD thy God; for thou hast fallen by thine iniquity. Take with you words, and turn to the Lord: say unto him, Take away all iniquity, and receive us graciously: so will we render the calves of our lips. Asshur shall not save us; we will not ride upon horses: neither will we say any more to the work of our hands, Ye are our gods: for in thee the fatherless findeth mercy.

I will heal their backsliding, I will love them freely: for mine anger is turned away from him. I will be as the dew unto Israel: he shall grow as the lily, and cast forth his roots as Lebanon. His branches shall spread, and his beauty shall be as the olive tree, and his smell as Lebanon (Hos. 14:1–6).

THERE ARE TWO QUESTIONS which, more than all others, agitate the bosom of a young believer:

Is it possible for one who has truly believed on Jesus ever to sin again?

If that be possible, is it possible for such a backslidden believer ever to be restored again to the light of God's countenance?

Now to both of these questions, the passage I have read returns a most complete answer. It shows plainly that it is possible for one who has believed in Jesus to sin again; and it shows that it is possible for that backslidden believer to be restored again to new peace and new holiness.

Let us go over the passage:

I. IT IS POSSIBLE FOR A BELIEVER TO SIN.

It is here said that Israel had fallen by their iniquity. 'O Israel, return unto the Lord thy God; for thou hast fallen by thine iniquity.' That God is here speaking to believers is evident, because He calls them by the name of Israel, the name of His peculiar people, and because He calls himself their God, which He would not have done if He had not been speaking to those who had once been made the children of God.

They had fallen from peace by their iniquity. When an awakened heart comes first to believe in Jesus, there is felt for the first time that calm and blessed state of mind which the Bible calls 'peace in believing'. Coming after a season of terror and anxiety it is like the surest calm that sometimes follows after a thunderstorm when the sun shines brightly through the last drops of the thunder shower, and the rainbow of the covenant is painted on the back of the retreating storm.

It is not then to be wondered at that, when there is spread for the first time this divine tranquillity through the believing bosom, when for the first time this heaven upon earth is realized in the once-anxious soul, the young believer should often imagine that heaven is already gained and that he has bid farewell to sin and sorrow for evermore.

When you introduce a man suddenly from the darkness of midnight, into the dazzling brilliance of a lighted apartment, it is not to be wondered at that he should at first be blinded and should make many a mistake as to the real position in which he stands.

O Israel, Return!

And just so when a soul is brought in from the worse than Egyptian darkness – a darkness that could be felt – of an unconverted mind, through the rent veil into the light of the reconciled countenance of Jehovah, to bask in the loving beams of that uncreated Sun, what wonder if the soul be dazzled and blinded? What wonder if like Peter on the Mount of Transfiguration, he should think that heaven is already gained and that there is no need of revisiting the bleak, unholy world any more.

But alas! this golden vision is too easily broken and it may need but the passing away of one little week, perhaps of one little day, to convince him that heaven is not yet gained; and that, though the Red Sea may be passed, there is a wide, howling wilderness to pass through and many an enemy to be overcome before the soul enters into the land where there is no sin and no sorrow.

You may have seen some bird of noble plumage rising from the earth on swift, careering wing; he leaves behind him the dull clods of the earth and soars to heaven as if it were his native element, when suddenly the whizzing bullet pierces his feathered side. On the instant all his noble energy is gone, he droops the head and covers the wing and whirling, falls from his dizzy height, down to the earth again. Just so the believer is exalted to heaven by the sweet peace wherewith the sprinkled blood has filled his soul, breathing a purer atmosphere, beginning now to think that heaven is gained; but suddenly the arrow of the Wicked One pierces his side and he falls. Ah! how low, who can tell?

Who can tell the misery of the believer's first sin? Before he felt himself within the veil, but now he feels he is turned out. Before he felt the warming beams of God's countenance upon his heart, but now he feels away from God. Before his heart was full in prayer, he said, 'Abba, Father', but now he dares not to raise his eyes to heaven, he dares not to say, 'Our Father'. Before, the Bible was his delight, the man of his counsels (*Psa.* 119:24, margin), his only bosom friend, now he almost shuns the sight of it. Before, the sight of Jesus gave him peace, but now he feels that he has wounded Him in the house of His friends, that he hath eaten bread with Him and yet lifted up the heel against Him, and therefore he dares not to look at Jesus.

Ah! is there one such poor soul that has thus been brought out of darkness, into still more marvellous darkness? Then you are this day a living evidence that it is possible for a believer to sin. You know the meaning of these words far better than I can explain them. 'O Israel, thou hast fallen by thine iniquity.' 'O Israel, thou hast destroyed thyself' (*Hos.* 13:9).

The believer falls from purity by his iniquity. When a branch is grafted into a vine, then, for the first time, does the juice of the vine flow into the bough, sweetening all and nourishing all. Just so, when a soul comes for the first time to believe in Jesus, he feels for the first time what it is to be made holy, to have the Spirit flowing into him, like a well of water springing up into everlasting life. He knows what he never knew before, that God works in the soul to will and to do of His good pleasure. Oh! who can tell the joy that fills the believing bosom when he finds out this, the grand secret of a holy life, when he finds holiness made easy, the way now all pleasantness and peace? He thinks perhaps that his foot shall never slip again, and if indeed he remained abiding in Jesus, he never would sin again!

But his faith fails and he falls. And oh! who can tell what a fall is there? It is not one sin only. It is like the tearing out the branch that has been newly grafted in; every stream of nourishing sap is cut off and it cannot but wither in every part. Just so when a believer sins, his union to the Saviour is mightily broken up, the flow of the Spirit into the heart is interrupted. Severed from Christ, he can do

O Israel, Return!

nothing. All his duties now are mere nothings, cold and formal blanks. He has no love to work for Christ. The well has ceased to spring within, and all his affections begin to wither. He ceases to spread around him the greenness of a vital godliness. Ah! is there one poor soul that has gone through this? Then you know it is possible for a believer to sin. You know by sad experience the meaning of the words, 'O Israel, thou hast fallen by thine iniquity.'

2. IT IS POSSIBLE FOR THE BACKSLIDDEN BELIEVER TO RETURN.

God is anxious that backslidden Israel should return. 'O Israel, return unto the LORD thy God!' In the words of our text, God not only beseeches a backslidden Israel to return, but he puts words into his mouth, actually shows him the very footsteps by which he is to return.

i. He is to Cast Away All Self-Confidence.

One would think that a soul that has once found its own righteousness to be filthy rags and once put on the divine righteousness of Jesus, would never ever again think of commending himself to God by anything of his own. One would think it would be a matter for ever settled and put to rest in the heart of every believer that, do what he could, he never could recommend himself to God, that his sin and misery are his only title to the love of Jesus.

But alas! self-righteousness is bred in the bone; it is like a constitutional disease that has come down from our father, Adam and our mother, Eve, who made themselves aprons. And even the believer who, but an hour ago, was casting contempt on his own righteousness and glorying only in the Redeemer's blessed garments, yet now, when he has fallen into sin, he begins the old story over again, begins to go about to establish his own righteousness and forgets altogether the righteousness of God. I appeal to every believing man who hears, when you have fallen into sin, is not the first and most natural struggle of your heart, to buy back the favour of God? When the first hour of sullenness and gloom has passed away, do you not set about, by a system of penances and performances, to recommend yourself once more to the Saviour? You feel that you dare not come to Jesus without making yourself somehow worthy of His regard by your tears and prayers. And if you have cried and prayed thus for some time, you think it hard that He does not come to restore you to peace and comfort again.

Ah! my friends, there is a deep deceit of the devil here. This is just leaning upon Asshur to save you, this is just depending on the swiftness of your horses, this is saying to the work of your hands, Ye are our gods. This is not coming fatherless. One who is truly fatherless is left destitute, an orphan without anything to recommend him.

How was it that you came to Jesus at first, when you were nothing but a sinner? Did your tears or penances recommend you to Jesus then? Or did He not rather love you before you shed a tear? Did He not die for you when you were a hardened enemy? Ah! then come to Jesus in the same way now, do not wait to make yourself better before you come. The longer you wait, you are only the worse.

Come, just because you are the chiefest of sinners; just because you have been so base as to dip the hand in the dish with Him and yet betray Him; just because you have been so unbelieving as to think that you must buy back an interest in His blood. Come and say, Asshur shall not save us; we will not ride upon horses: neither will we say any more to the work of our hands, Ye are our gods. We will not trust in our tears or penances, for in Thee the fatherless findeth mercy.

O Israel, Return!

ii. He Is to Come Seeking Complete Restoration.

When two women came before Solomon, each claiming to be the mother of a living child, it showed what deep knowledge of human nature the Spirit of God had given him when he decided that the woman who would let the child be halved was not the mother, and that she who would have the whole child or none was indeed the mother.

It is just so with the backslidden believer. He who comes with prayers and tears and penances to buy the forgiveness of sins, he has no true knowledge of the gospel way, and therefore he would be content with half of Christ, he would be content with half the privileges of the believer. He prays, 'Take away all iniquity', but forgets to say, 'Receive us graciously.' But the true believer, when he has fallen into sin, comes back with his eye fixed on the whole finished work of Christ. He finds himself fatherless, destitute of any power to recommend himself to God, therefore he accepts the full Christ as He is freely offered to sinners. He will not be content with half of Christ, will not be content with *forgiveness* without *acceptance* also.

He looks also to the finished obedience of Christ and cries out, 'Receive us graciously.' Receive us not only as those who have never sinned, but as those who have done Thy law and delighted to do it.

Oh! my friends, do you know anything of coming to God in this bold and blessed way? If not, you have never yet understood the gospel and all our preaching has been in vain. We might as well have been telling you about some fairy islands in the sea, where the flowers are always blossoming and the trees are ever bearing fruit, where the inhabitants never say that they are sick and where love and joy for ever reign! You never will come to these fairy islands because they are nowhere to be found, and you will not come to the peace and joy of those whose iniquity is all taken away and on whom God smiles graciously, because you will not listen to us when we tell you that the way to come to God is not by making yourselves better but by looking unto Jesus.

3. GOD RECEIVES THE RETURNING BACKSLIDER MORE KINDLY THAN EVER.

He says, 'I will heal their backsliding.' He shows His renewed kindness in two ways more wonderful than the believer can ask or think.

i. 'I WILL LOVE HIM FREELY.'

As long as the believer remains in the Holiest of all, he dwells under the beams of that God who is love. God's face shines full upon him, and it is all love. But when he sins he feels banished out of the tabernacle; he walks round and round it in gloom and sadness. No ray of Jehovah's love can reach his heart.

But then he bethinks him of the rent veil, that it was rent from the top to the bottom, that it was rent for sinners, even the chief, that, vile and hateful sinner though he be, he cannot be a greater sinner than the chief, he cannot be too great a sinner to find free access by Jesus once more to the Father. Then faith springs up anew in his heart.

He opens his Bible to make sure that he does not mistake and he finds it written, 'I am the door: by me if any man enter in, he shall be saved, and shall go in and out, and find pasture' (*John* 10:9). He thanks God and takes courage, enters once more through the rent veil and finds it is all true. Jesus is the way to the Father, and as he stands beneath the reconciled face of God, he hears these words, 'I will heal thy backsliding; I will love thee freely: for Mine anger is turned away from thee.'

Ah! my believing friends, do you remember what Jude says, 'Keep yourselves in the love of God' (*Jude* 21). Abide in Jesus, and then you shall abide in His love. If there was one spot upon the face of the earth where God's love was always abiding and shining, oh! what would you not give that you might dwell there all the days of your life? How it would sweeten all your sorrows and hallow all your joys. Ah! my friends, there is such a spot within reach of you all, offered without money and without price, and that spot is JESUS. In Him the Father is ever well-pleased.

Abide in Him and then the Father will be ever well-pleased with you. And if it be good and pleasant to be loved by a friend on earth, ah! who can tell the blessedness of being beloved by our Father in heaven. Earthly friends will fail, earthly friends will forsake thee, but Jehovah will never fail thee. Jehovah will never forsake thee. Recline then, in the bosom of Jesus, that you may rest in the bosom of God.

ii. 'I WILL BE AS THE DEW UNTO ISRAEL.'

God not only pours his free love down on the returned backslider, He pours down his Spirit also.

a. Those of you who have watched the falling of the dew know well that it only falls when the sun has gone down, leaving a calm clear sky, undarkened by clouds and unagitated by the wind. Just so, it is only when the backslidden believer has come again to some peace in believing, when he has come again into the love of God and says, 'Return unto thy rest, O my soul'; it is then when the believer's sky is clear, undarkened by one breath of anxiety, for God loves him freely: it is then that the dew of the Spirit descends upon the soul. Oh! do you know anything of these ways of God?

b. The dew always descends unfelt, unseen, unheard. No man can tell whence it cometh or whither it goeth. So is every one that is born of the Spirit. We do not bid you look out for miracles, wonders in the heaven above or in the earth beneath; we do not bid you seek for sudden impulses and raptures carrying you into the third heaven. God could give you these too if they were good for you. But what He promises here to the returned backslider, to all of you who will come fatherless to hide in the wounds of Jesus, is that He will be like the dew unto your souls. He will come in an hour and way when you think not, silently but surely. Reckon then upon this help. Go boldly forward counting upon it, to every duty, to every trial. Though He tarry, wait for Him, for He will come and will not tarry.

c. Wherever the dew falls, there it moistens everything, it leaves not one leaf unmoistened, there is not a tiny blade of grass on which its diamond drops do not descend. Every leaf and stem of the bush is heavy with the dewy load. Just so is the divine dew on the soul. There is not a faculty, there is not an affection, a power, or passion of the soul, on which the Spirit does not descend. Oh! how you mistake the matter, then, if you think that some small outward reformation is the evidence of the Spirit's work. No, my friends, the dew comes upon every leaf, the Spirit comes upon every thought and feeling of the inner man; and unless you be led, *led* by the Spirit of Christ, you are none of His. If any man be in Christ Jesus he is a new creature.

d. The dew makes all things fruitful and draws forth the fragrance from every flower. And so here, 'I will be as the dew unto Israel.' Just as the dew is the nourisher of every green thing, causing every plant to bloom and blossom and every tree to cast forth its roots, the branches to spread and the beauty to revive and, above all, as

O Israel, Return!

the dew calls forth all the fragrance of the flowers, so does the Spirit, descending on the heart of the returned believer, revive the whole soul and call forth every fragrant affection of the heart. The soul grows fair and upright like the lily, the roots of faith cast themselves deeper and wider, like the very cedars of Lebanon.

The believer's new affections, like branches, spread out far and wide. His beauty is like the olive tree and the fragrance of his good deeds is like the fragrance from the Vales of Lebanon.

Oh! my believing friends, where is the evidence that this dew is mightily descending upon you? Are you growing like the lily? Are you spreading out your roots like Lebanon? Have you grown any, since we came among you? The fields around you have been ploughed and sown, the crops have risen, and are now white with the harvest, ready to be gathered in. And is there no advance in your souls, no marks of the dew? Ah! what proof have we then that we have not run in vain and laboured in vain?

19

Trust Not in a Friend

> *Trust ye not in a friend, put ye not confidence in a guide: keep the doors of thy mouth from her that lieth in thy bosom. For the son dishonoureth the father, the daughter riseth up against her mother, the daughter in law against her mother in law; a man's enemies are the men of his own house. Therefore I will look unto the* LORD; *I will wait for the God of my salvation: my God will hear me* (Mic. 7:5–7).

PART OF THESE WORDS from the prophecy of Micah were made use of by Christ when he sent out his twelve as sheep in the midst of wolves (*Matt.* 10:16–42).

In that discourse, our Saviour was imparting encouragement to his disciples. They did not need to take thought how or what they would speak. It would be given them at the time what to speak. In this respect they would be like Christ Himself. Moreover, they were the objects of their heavenly Father's care. 'The very hairs of your head are all numbered' (*Matt.* 10:30).

However, they were not to think that He had come to bring peace. There would be division because of Him. He quotes the prophecy of Micah for two reasons:

1. To teach them not to expect that whole families would turn. Their preaching would produce division even within families.

Their converts would often need to love Christ more than father or mother.

2. For their own sakes, to teach them that they must not trust in friends in their hour of need, but in Christ.

These words doubtless applied to Israel at the time. Good men then were scarce, like fruit when the gathering is past, like grapes when the vintage is done, scarce one left. The best of men was as a briar, the most upright sharper than a thorn hedge (*Mic.* 7:4). Friends, husband, wife, were not to be trusted. Son, daughter, daughter-in-law, might all be enemies. The godly man in such a time is driven away from human friendship to wait for God. 'Therefore I will look unto the LORD; I will wait for the God of my salvation: my God will hear me' (*Mic.* 7:7). With what a sweet and humble confidence he says, 'My God will hear me'!

These words also apply in all times when the gospel is preached. It is as true now as ever it was. 'I came not to send peace, but a sword' (*Matt.* 10:34).

The doctrine I would draw from this is that we should not look to worldly friends for help, but wait on God, saying, 'My God will hear me.'

I would chiefly apply this to persons awakened to seek salvation in Christ; and to them I would say:

1. THINK IT NOT STRANGE IF YOUR NEAREST FRIENDS OPPOSE YOU.

When a soul that has lain in the bosom of a godless family and among godless friends is awakened by reading the Bible or under the preaching of Word, you would think all would feel for him. If he met with an accident, or fell sick, everyone would run and sit by his bedside. But if he drops a tear upon his Bible; if he trembles under the Word; if the soul be stricken through and through, as with a dart; if terrors of wrath go over his soul: not a drop of sympathy is found in any bosom. It dries up even the milk of kindness in a mother's breast. The husband has no pity. The wife no tender sympathy. 'A man's enemies are the men of his own house.' But do not think it strange. It was so in the days of Micah. It was so in the days of Jesus. It will be to the end. You see it well portrayed in Bunyan's *The Pilgrim's Progress*. Do not conclude from it that something must be wrong.

2. YOU ARE NOT TO SEEK HELP FROM WORLDLY FRIENDS.

You are not to trust in a friend. You are not to put confidence in a guide. You are to keep the doors of your mouth from your own wife. I know not where one so readily goes for help as to nature's counsellors. Every family is like a little council of peace and war. Every scheme is debated in the family circle. Every pleasure is devised there, plans of fortune and of fame. What this son is to be, and that.

Or if you go beyond the family circle, it is to the intimate friend, the constant companion. Those that walk together, and play together, and unbosom secrets to one another, how likely it is that when the soul is awakened it should go to these. 'Trust not.' 'Put not confidence.' 'Keep the doors of thy mouth.' This is the only subject that cannot be brought into the circle of the godless family. It will rend it in pieces. It will bring in the frown, the taunt, the angry word, the silent tear. A man's foes shall be they of his own house. It cannot be trusted to a friend. It will rend that friendship for ever asunder.

When you bring fire and water together, there cannot be peace. Bring a work of grace among natural hearts, it explodes immediately. I may be speaking to someone who knows this in sad experience. Some feel it most bitterly. Why must it be so? Because, if worldly friends wept with you and sympathized with you, you would soon say, 'Peace, peace.' You would be contented to remain like them. You would seek no pardon. But when you are driven from them, you are forced to seek a true peace. Opposition drives us to seek relief from God alone.

I would take occasion from this to speak to worldly people. Surely this should convince you of the bad state you are in, that those truly awakened to seek God should obtain nothing but opposition from you. But then this will also drive us all from help in man. If those that love us best will not help us, then none will – none but our God.

3. LOOK UNTO THE LORD.

'I will wait for the God of my salvation: my God will hear me.' These words display a lovely, self-emptying confidence.

i. It Is from the Lord that Their Distress Comes.

If He had allowed them to live as they were, they would have been unawakened, nay, they would have been persecutors. If grace had chosen any other member of the family, they would have opposed them. God has revealed their lost condition, by a work of Almighty power. Be convinced of this. It is not an enemy that has wounded you.

ii. Awakened Souls Should Quietly Wait on God.

They feel their lost condition. As they look around, they feel without a friend. But while they feel desolate, they feel it would be just in God to leave them for ever thus. The awakened soul does not murmur. Then, if ever, your God will hear you. Some strive to make themselves righteous; some to bring themselves to believe. Some look and wait for a change in themselves. But wait for the God of your salvation.

I will also apply the words of the text to believers in distress and in soul trouble.

1. *Think it not strange if the world does not understand;* if it mocks; if it opposes you. It is always so in soul troubles. When a soul is walking in darkness and has no light, the world has no compassion. They differ from God in this. The dearest friends, if of the world, do not, *cannot* comprehend your sorrow.

2. *Expect no light from the world.* If a man's lamp went out, would he go to the dark night to light it? If you have lost the comfort that was in your soul, do you think to warm yourself in the cold, dead bosom of the world? 'Trust not in a friend.'

3. *Expect no light from the children of God.* They are often instruments, but if you go to them as fountains, you will find them dry. It is strange how much readier darkened souls are to go to books and Christians than to Christ. 'Trust not in a friend.' They may be sweet channels, but they are not fountains. They shine only with borrowed light.

4. *Look to the Lord.* 'I will wait for the God of my salvation: my God will hear me.' Take God for your God, even in the dark. Say to Christ, 'Thy God shall be my God.' If He seems to delay, do not count delay refusal. Say still, 'Lord, help me.' Add prayer to your waiting. Do not lose this confidence, 'My God *will* hear me.'

20

A Pure Language

For then will I turn to the people a pure language, that they may all call upon the name of the LORD, *to serve him with one consent. From beyond the rivers of Ethiopia my suppliants, even the daughter of my dispersed, shall bring mine offering. In that day shalt thou not be ashamed for all thy doings, wherein thou hast transgressed against me: for then I will take away out of the midst of thee them that rejoice in thy pride, and thou shalt no more be haughty because of my holy mountain* (Zeph. 3:9–11).

THE PROPHECY IN THIS PLACE concerning a pure language, with which to call upon the name of the Lord, is clearly a promise concerning the times of the gospel. Isaiah, too, spoke of a time when five cities in the land of Egypt would speak the language of Canaan (*Isa.* 19:18). Before God confounded the language of the earth at the tower of Babel, the whole earth was of one language, or, as the Hebrew says, of one lip (*Gen.* 11:1), but that was not used to glorify God. Now, in the time of the gospel, the apostle prays that the church may, with one mind and one mouth, glorify God, and that the Gentiles might glorify God for His mercy (*Rom.* 15:6, 9).

The mention also of Ethiopia in verse 10 reminds us of the time spoken of in Psalm 68:31 when Ethiopia would stretch out her hands to God. The time would also come when the Lord would recover the remnant of His people from Cush, which is Ethiopia (*Isa.* 11:11); and Isaiah 49 shows that the Gentiles would gather round the restored Jews, bringing them in their arms and on their shoulders, and Gentile kings and queens should nurse them. Isaiah 60 speaks of the same times.

The time prophesied of was to be a time when shame would be forgotten (*Zeph.* 3:11), and when God would bring praise and fame to His people where they had been put to shame before (verses 19 and 20). This is in harmony with what is said by Isaiah, 'Ye shall not be ashamed nor confounded world without end' (*Isa.* 45:17), and, 'Thou shalt forget the shame of thy youth' (*Isa.* 54:4); for, 'Whosoever believeth in him (Christ) shall not be ashamed' (*Rom.* 9:33), or 'confounded' (*1 Pet.* 2:6).

Pride and haughtiness were also to be put away (*Zeph.* 3:11). How often the prophets had to admonish Israel not to trust in outward privileges: 'Trust ye not in lying words, saying, The temple of the LORD, the temple of the LORD, the temple of the LORD, are these' (*Jer.* 7:4). 'Is not the LORD among us?', said Israel in presumption, 'None evil can come upon us' (*Mic.* 3:11). Again in later times they trusted that they had Abraham for their father (*Matt.* 3:9), and that being a Jew outwardly was sufficient, as we see in Romans, chapter 2. But then God would bring about a great change, sending the gospel of His grace to the nations and to a remnant of Israel.

As it reads literally, 'For then I will change the lips of the nations and give them a pure language', that they may all call upon the name of the Saviour, with the cry of faith. Then they would serve Him, doing His will, drawing His easy yoke as with one shoulder. From beyond the rivers of Ethiopia His praying people would come, and the daughter of His dispersed Israel would bring His offering. Then the words of our text would be fulfilled.

A Pure Language

In our text, God says, in effect, 'In that day shalt thou not be ashamed for all thy past sins. Thou shalt see them carried away in Christ, forgotten, blotted out. And thou shalt be a new creature. Thy proud children shall be gone, and thou shalt no more be haughty in my holy mountain, or because of my holy mountain. No more wilt thou say, The temple of the LORD are these, or, I am holier than thou.'

At first sight, Ezekiel 16:63 seems to contradict our text, speaking as it does of *remembering* and *being ashamed*. But there is no real contradiction.

1. When a believer looks to himself, to his past life, he is dumb, he is ashamed. This is the look spoken of by Ezekiel.

2. When a believer looks to Christ for full pardon, he cannot be ashamed. 'My tongue shall sing aloud of thy righteousness.'

In the latter day, God will give the nations the language of faith, the same language, the same yoke. His ancient people shall become a praying people and shall come to Him from all countries. They shall not be ashamed, either of their idolatries, their crucifying Christ, or their long unbelief. They shall see the sin all pardoned, and so have no feelings of guilt or shame. They shall no more be a haughty people but meek, and poor, and trusting in the Lord. Let us learn from this:

1. GOD IS THE AUTHOR OF CONVERSION.

'I will turn to the people a pure language.' God will change the language of the nations to a language of faith.

2. WHEN GOD CHANGES THE HEART HE CHANGES THE LANGUAGE.

There is no more idle talk, lasciviousness, malicious swearing. 'I will turn to them a pure language that they may all call upon the name of the LORD.' Their first cry is, 'What must I do to be saved?' And their second cry is, 'My Lord, and my God!' There is a wonderful sameness in all converted persons. The language of the unconverted is like Babel, confused, each different, but the language of grace alone unites men. They 'serve him with one consent', literally 'one shoulder', like beasts in the same yoke.

3. ISRAEL SHALL NOT BE ASHAMED FOR ALL THEIR SINS.

When souls are brought into Christ, they have no more cause of shame. The unconverted have no shame. They have a whore's forehead. They cannot blush. But the awakened soul is covered over with shame, like the publican in the parable (*Luke* 18:9–14).

Even Christians are filled with shame, when they look only on themselves and what they have been (*Ezek.* 16:63). But when they look to Christ, their shame is forgotten. There are two reasons:

i. Their sins, they see, are fully accounted for in the sufferings of Christ; more fully than if they themselves had suffered eternally.

ii. They see that they are righteous in God's sight, that God loves them – how can they be ashamed any more? They have 'no more conscience of sins' (*Heb.* 10:2), like those in heaven who have washed their robes in the blood of the Lamb (*Rev.* 7:14). They remember their sins, but they are not ashamed. The reproach is wiped off forever. Even here, insofar as you live by faith, you may live without shame.

They are no more haughty. Israel are proud now. But, when restored, they will not be haughty, but meek and poor in spirit, trusting in God. All the unconverted are haughty. They will not submit to Christ. Saul was proud. So was Zacchaeus. So was the Philippian jailor. Only apprehend Christ, and then the promise is sure, 'Thou shalt no more be haughty' (*Zeph.* 3:11).

21

The Candlestick and the Olive Trees[1]

And [he] said unto me, What seest thou? And I said, I have looked, and behold a candlestick all of gold, with a bowl upon the top of it, and his seven lamps thereon, and seven pipes to the seven lamps, which are upon the top thereof: And two olive trees by it, one upon the right side of the bowl, and the other upon the left side thereof. So I answered and spake to the angel that talked with me, saying, What are these, my lord? Then the angel that talked with me answered and said unto me, Knowest thou not what these be? And I said, No, my lord. Then he answered and spake unto me, saying, This is the word of the LORD unto Zerubbabel, saying, Not by might, nor by power, but by my spirit, saith the LORD of hosts (Zech. 4:2–6).

ZERUBBABEL WAS ONE OF THE PRINCES OF JUDAH when the Jews were in captivity. He was commissioned by Cyrus to build again the temple in Jerusalem which had lain waste for nearly seventy years. Accordingly he returned to his native land with a number of his fellow-captives and laid the foundation of the Lord's house in troubled times. He was much discouraged, first by one enemy and then by another, till the work was actually stopped. But God sent Haggai and Zechariah to encourage him and the people in the work. This vision of Zechariah was intended for this purpose.

[1] Preached in St Peter's, Dundee, 24 September 1837.

ZECHARIAH'S VISION

He saw a golden candlestick, very much the same as that which used to be in the temple before it was burned. It had a golden bowl upon the top for holding oil. From this golden bowl seven pipes conducted the oil to the seven lamps or burners of the candlestick. All this was plain enough. But he saw greater things than these. Two olive trees grew close beside the candlestick, one on the right hand, the other on the left. From these two olive trees two branches laden with olive berries hung over the candlestick and so full were they with enriching oil that without being pressed or squeezed by the hands of man, they emptied themselves, poured the rich golden oil into the receiver of the candlestick. In this way the lamps received a never-ending supply of oil. Let us try and understand these things.

1. THE CANDLESTICK REPRESENTS THE CHURCH.

So it was in the Jewish Temple long ago. In the holy place there was the golden candlestick, a constant type of the church of God and it was the task of the priests to keep it lighted day by day. So in the Revelation chapter 1, John saw the church represented by seven golden candlesticks, and Christ as the priest walking among them to keep them burning and lighted day by day. So here we have the same type of a candlestick with seven lamps representing the church.

A candlestick is intended to give light; so is the church. This world is a dark world. To unconverted people, this world appears full of light, but every one that has had his eyes opened feels that this is a dark, a very dark world. He feels that he was sitting in darkness and in the shadow of death. He sees that men love the darkness rather than the light, because their deeds are evil. Now though this be a dark world, yet God has raised up lights in it. He hath set up a candlestick in it, in order to give light. Ah! the people of God are the only light thing in this dark world. Now every believer is a lamp of this candlestick, a burning and a shining light, lighted by God, kept burning by Him in order to give light.

i. ARE YOU A BELIEVER?

Remember you are a lamp of this great candlestick. You are set in a conspicuous situation. You are intended to give light. 'Ye are the light of the world. A city that is set on a hill cannot be hid. Neither do men light a candle, and put it under a bushel, but on a candlestick; and it giveth light to all that are in the house. Let your light so shine before men, that they may see your good works, and glorify your Father which is in heaven' (*Matt.* 5:15–16).

Learn from this how wrong it is to hide your light. Some Christians are worse than Nicodemus. He came to Jesus by night the first time he came. But they come to Him always by night. Some Christians are ashamed to show that they are Christians; some lamps are afraid to shine. Some hog the gospel to themselves, and feast on it in secret, but they do not display anything of their joy to the dearest friend they have on earth. They hold their hands round the candle lest any should see. Ah! there is something wrong here. No lamp is lighted for its own enjoyment, but to give light. If a candle does not give light, it should be put out. Why did God make you a Christian? Was it not that you might shine?

ii. SOME SHINE ABROAD, BUT NOT AT HOME.

There is something wrong here. Some Christians blaze away when they are in company, and speak much of grace and glory, but at home they are like a dying lamp, flickering with uncertain light that does no good. Some such may be hearing me. There is something wrong here. A candle shines best of all in a room, and so a true heaven-lighted Christian should shine brightest in his own home. Correct this, I beseech of you! If you can preach like Paul in the world, and yet forget to teach your children and servants at home, then I stand in doubt of you. There is more of nature than of grace in that blaze.

iii. LEARN TO SHINE TOGETHER.

When a lonely candle is brought into a large dark room it looks dismal indeed. It only seems to make the darkness visible. So is it when Christians shine singly and alone in this world. They only make the darkness visible. Christians join together! Be a candlestick with seven lamps. Agree together to pray, strive together, speak often one to another; and thus you will cheer one another and dispel the gloom.

2. THE CANDLESTICK WAS OF GOLD, THE MOST PRECIOUS METAL.

The candlestick in the temple was of pure gold, and so were the seven candlesticks which John saw, 'golden candlesticks' (*Rev.* 1:12). This shows the preciousness of Christ's church. The people of Christ are the precious metal of the world. In every great house there are vessels of gold and of silver, of wood and of stone. Now, believers are vessels of gold in Christ. Believers are like precious metal:

i. BECAUSE THEY ARE REDEEMED AT SO GREAT A PRICE.

They are redeemed with no corruptible thing, such as silver and gold, but with the precious blood of Christ. How precious hell-deserving sinners must have been in the eyes of God! Justice said, 'Cut them down; why cumber they the ground?' But God's hand was searching amid all the precious things of the universe. At last

The Candlestick and the Olive Trees

He laid His hand upon His own Son, the pearl of great price, and said, 'Deliver [them] from going down to the pit: I have found a ransom' (*Job* 33:24). Have you been thus ransomed? Ah, think then how precious you are, not in yourself, but in the price that was paid for you. You are gold.

ii. BECAUSE THE NATURE OF BELIEVERS IS CHANGED.

In their natural state, they were dust and ashes, ready to be dashed into pieces. 'Reprobate silver shall men call them, for the LORD hath rejected them' (*Jer.* 6:30). But brought into Christ Jesus they are created again in Him, their nature is changed, they are made partakers of the divine nature, they are moulded and fashioned into a golden candlestick to give light in the world. Are you a believer? Ah! then, your nature has been changed. You have become precious metal now, a new creature in Christ Jesus.

3. THE TWO OLIVE TREES REPRESENT OUR LORD JESUS CHRIST.

Why is Christ represented by two olive trees? Because they were types of Joshua, the high priest, and Zerubbabel, the governor, who were, in that day, God's instruments to build the temple; and they in turn were types of Christ in His two great offices, Priest and King, the great builder of His own temple.

i. THE CHURCH IS SUPPLIED OUT OF A LIVING SAVIOUR.

Never was a candlestick so wonderfully supplied with oil as was this candlestick. Other lamps have a reservoir full of oil, and when that is used up it must be supplied by the hand of man; but here, a living Olive Tree drops its golden oil into the oil vessels with a constant dripping: living oil from the living tree. If there are any Christians hearing me, I am sure your hearts must be full when you think of it. We have no dead Saviour. He is alive for evermore. And, 'Because I live, ye shall live also.' The world draws its pleasures out of dead reservoirs, broken cisterns that can hold no water; and when they are empty, they need to go to another, and then to another. Not so you who are Christians. You are supplied from a living tree, from a living Saviour. How is it that some Christians give such a flickering light? Ah, it is because you do not believe in the living Saviour! You are fearful, you are anxious about tomorrow, because you do not give God credit when he tells you that Christ is risen, full of the Spirit for his people. Ask and ye shall receive. Oh! live upon the fullness of that Olive Tree.

ii. How Near Christ Is to the Church.

Observe, the two olive trees stood close by the candlestick, the one on the right and the other on the left; and the branches hung over it so as to drop their oil into the golden pipes. So near is Christ to His own people. He is on their right hand, and on their left hand. He is about them and around them, and His branches are over them. They sit under the apple tree, and his fruit is sweet to their taste. In the Revelation, He is described as walking amidst the seven golden candlesticks. 'But if He be walking, then He may go away.' Nay, but look, here He is described as planted firm and fast beside his church. So true is that promise, 'I will not leave you orphans: I will come to you' (*John* 14:18 [margin]), 'Where two or three are gathered together in my name, there am I in the midst of them.' 'Lo, I am with you alway, even unto the end of the world.' Israel is a people near to Him, and He a Saviour near to them.

Some are afraid lest Christ should leave them. See here, He is a rooted tree close by His people. Fear not, He will never leave thee nor forsake thee. 'When thou passest through the waters, I will be with thee' (*Isa.* 43:2).

The Candlestick and the Olive Trees

Some think that Christ is gone from them. Some are asking, 'Saw ye him whom my soul loveth? I once sat under his shadow and tasted of His fruit and was nourished by His Spirit, but alas, he has left me and I am deserted.' Here, Christ is a planted tree. He has not left you. It is you that have left Him. Come once more under the branches of that good Olive Tree.

iii. How Freely, Constantly, Secretly Christ Gives His Spirit.

a. *How freely.*

It is expressly said that the branches emptied the golden oil out of themselves (Zech. 4:12). No human hand was needed to squeeze the olive berries. The full berries of themselves gave forth the golden oil, and the full stream ran into the golden bowl to feed the seven lamps of the candlestick. Such is the free Spirit given to all them that believe. 'If any man thirst let him come unto me and drink.'

Christians, what would become of you if Christ did not give the Spirit so liberally? If He waited till you squeezed the berries by the hand of prayer, ah, how often you would let Him wait till you were dry and the lamp out! But freely, sovereignly, and before you pray, He pours down the rich oil. It is a shower that tarries not for man, and waits not for the sons of men.

b. *How constantly.*

There is every reason to believe that the branches kept up a continual stream of oil into the lamps, so constant is the supply of the Spirit. 'I will give you another Comforter that He may abide with you forever.' Christians, do you know what you possess? The Spirit dwelling in you forever, the constant inflowing of the divine Spirit.

Then, be happy. Be not anxious for the future. Trust God to fulfil His Word. Be constantly doing the Lord's work. A lamp that is constantly fed should be constantly burning. Christ never wearies of pouring the Spirit into your heart. You should never weary in well-doing.

c. *How secretly.*

It is hardly possible to imagine a more secret and quiet way of feeding a lamp than that which the prophet saw when the olive berries so gently emptied themselves into the golden pipes. So secret, so gentle is the work of the Spirit in the hearts of believers. Oh! dear Christians, the world cannot receive Him because it seeth Him not, neither knoweth Him, but ye know Him, for He dwelleth with you and shall be in you.

How silently the dew falls in a still evening when not a breath of wind stirs the leaves. How silently a well of water springs up from the bowels of the earth. How secretly the wandering wind bloweth where it listeth. How secretly the oil dropped from the olive branches to supply the lamps. But more secretly, more silently than all, does the Spirit descend into the hearts of Christ's people.

A closing word to Christ's people, and to unbelievers:

Be not faithless, but believing. Trust to the Spirit, though you see Him not. Oh! how happily you would live if this vision were always in your mind. Be led by the Spirit, walk after the Spirit, and ye shall not fulfil the lusts of the flesh.

Even now is this Olive Tree dropping its sweet oil in this house of God, even now is it comforting and refreshing some hearts in the midst of us, perhaps some very poor person, or some very ignorant ill-educated person, but yet a part of the golden candlestick. Oh! how much happier that person is than you, if you are unconverted. He is a temple of the Holy Ghost. You are a cage of unclean birds. He has the earnest of heaven. You have the earnest of hell.

22

Not by Might, Nor by Power

*Then he answered and spake unto me, saying, This is the word of the
LORD unto Zerubbabel, saying, Not by might, nor by power, but by
my Spirit, saith the LORD of hosts* (Zech. 4:6).

ON ANOTHER OCCASION we considered the vision of the prophet Zechariah to which these words apply, the vision of the golden candlestick fed by the two olive trees. We saw that the candlestick represented the church of God, fed freely, constantly, yet secretly with the golden oil of the Spirit by the Lord Jesus Christ, represented in His offices of Priest and King by the two olive trees. We come now to apply these words in particular, 'This is the word of the LORD unto Zerubbabel, saying, Not by might, nor by power, but by my Spirit, saith the LORD of hosts' (*Zech.* 4:6).

1. CONVERSION IS NOT BY MIGHT, NOR BY POWER.

These words apply to the conversion of souls, in that conversion is not accomplished by might, nor by power, but by the Spirit of God. Though means are used to bring about conversion, yet it is not by the might of these means, but by the Spirit working through them, that souls are converted to God.

a. *This is true of the reading of the Word*. Many read the Word without feeling any effect, yet in the hands of the Spirit the Word cuts to the soul, 'piercing even to the dividing asunder of soul and spirit, joints and marrow, and is a discerner of the thoughts and intents of the heart' (*Heb.* 4:12).

b. *It is true of the preaching of the Word*. The preaching of the Word has no effect on most, yet in the hands of the Spirit it awakens many, and brings others who hear it to peace.

We may learn from this consideration:

i. *To be diligent in the use of means*.

Though we do not place confidence in the means, yet it is by them that God is often pleased to work.

ii. *To continue to hope for a revival*.

If it were by might or by power, then we might indeed droop. Where are all mighty men now? Where is Paul now? Where now is an Apollos, mighty in the Scriptures? Where now are Knox and Melville? Where is Richard Cameron? Where is William Guthrie now? But it is not by might, nor by power. Though we have few men of power in our day, yet if we have men of prayer they will bring down the Spirit.

iii. *To learn how the best means have often failed*.

Even when Christ preached, many heard unmoved. It was so when Paul preached at Athens. So it is in our day. There is much faithful preaching, yet little effect. Why? It is 'not by might, nor by power, but by my Spirit'. There is a withholding of the Spirit.

2. SANCTIFICATION IS NOT BY MIGHT, NOR BY POWER.

In the sanctification of the people of God, though means are used, yet the work is not by might, nor by power, but by God's Spirit. There are mountains in the way. The natural heart is like a great mountain. It is the *Hill Difficulty*. How can I believe? How can I persevere? How can I overcome? But, 'Who art thou, O great mountain? before Zerubbabel thou shalt become a plain: and he shall bring forth the headstone thereof with shoutings, crying, Grace, grace unto it' (*Zech.* 4:7). The mountain will become a plain before the soul, because God's Spirit fills the heart. God has two ways of enabling us to overcome:

a. *He makes our feet like hinds' feet.* He enables us to run and not be weary, to climb up the mountain, and it becomes a Nebo, a height from which to view the promised land.

b. *He makes the mountain become a plain.* Then the soul runs in the way of God's commandments. Faith takes the mountain quite away. In such ways the mountain becomes nothing, because of the Spirit of God continually dripping into the soul, as in the vision of the prophet here.

From these things I would have Christians learn:

i. *Not to faint in the hour of temptation.*
I know there are mountains in your way, but live by faith, not by sight. Live as if you saw that Olive Tree, always dripping golden oil into the golden bowl to feed the golden lamps.

ii. *Not to faint from the opposition of the world.*
This too is a mountain in your way, but live by faith. It shall become a plain.

iii. *Not to faint in the hour of adversity.*
How often adversity is taken away and becomes a plain, or, if not, it becomes a vantage point from which to gaze into glory.

3. GLORIFICATION IS NOT BY MIGHT, NOR BY POWER.

Your bodies are the temples of the Holy Ghost. Every day Christ is laying down more costly gold in the temple. The day will come when He will finish it, when He will lay on the top stone, and present you to Himself. Now, all this will be not by might, nor by human power, but by his Spirit working in you.

i. At Death.

At death, Christ lays the top stone on the structure. Now it is not by might, now it is not by human power, that you can go through that awful scene. It is by God's Spirit. God keeps dying strength in store for a dying hour. He will carry all His people, if not triumphantly, at least safely through. And when the soul lifts itself up in paradise, these words shall be sung by the angels, 'Grace, grace unto it!' 'O death, where is thy sting? O grave, where is thy victory?' (1 Cor. 15:55).

ii. At the Resurrection.

Then Christ's whole temple will be complete. Ah, eternal monuments of grace! They will be there, not by might, nor by power. But this far surpasses all I can say or think. Oh, may we all be found living stones of that great temple!

It is not by human power, but by God's Spirit, that souls are saved, and sanctified, that God's church is built up on earth, and finally brought to eternal glory.

23

The Lord Hearkening to His People[1]

Then they that feared the LORD spake often one to another: and the LORD hearkened and heard it, and a book of remembrance was written before him for them that feared the LORD, and that thought upon his name (Mal. 3:16).

THE FIRST THING I desire you to observe in this passage is the descriptions which are here given of the children of God. They are those who 'feared the Lord', and who 'thought upon His name'. In all generations these will be found to be the distinguishing marks of all believers.

1. THEY ARE FEARERS OF THE LORD.

This is an expression which occurs constantly in the Bible and which it may be well once for all to explain. There are two kinds of fear mentioned in the Bible:

i. *One is the fear of terror which is said to have torment.* This is the fear which newly awakened sinners have when they find 'the sorrows of death compassing them and the pains of hell getting hold on

---

[1] Preached in Carronshore, Plean, Dunipace, and in St Peter's, Dundee, in 1837.

them'. There is no sign of a believer in Jesus in this fear. The moment a man becomes a believer in Jesus, he begins to lose this fear, which has torment. And when he comes to perfect love, then perfect love casts out this fear. This is the fear which devils have when they believe and tremble. Instead of being the temper of holy and happy beings, it is the very temper of devils. It is next door to hatred. It is the very atmosphere of hell.

ii. *But the fear of the Lord of which the text speaks is the very beginning of wisdom,* or as the margin renders it, 'the sum of wisdom'. It is a feeling which the humblest believer on the earth shares with the highest seraphim before the throne, who veil their faces with their wings while they cry one to another, 'Holy, Holy, Holy.' This fear, which may be called the fear of love in opposition to the fear of terror, is a compound feeling made up of holy love and holy awe.

Could I lift away from the eyes of any of you that veil, whatever it is, that now covers you; could I show you fully and plainly how God hath loved you so as to send Jesus to die for you; could I show you how His bowels yearned over your perishing souls, when He saw that you were all lying under the curse, all worthy only of hell; could I show how Jesus has loved you; how He has followed you ever since you were a child; how His hand has kept you out of hell to this day; how He has tracked your every footstep in every haunt of pleasure, in every haunt of sin, while you asked not for Him, cared not for Him; could I make you suddenly turn round as it were, and see the Good Shepherd – even at this moment – seeking you, the lost sheep, offering you His own blood and His own righteousness, that you might not perish but have everlasting life – if I could only do this, which I cannot do, I am quite sure that no sooner would your eye fall upon that loving Saviour than your rocky heart would melt. Although your heart be like the millstone, although you never

The Lord Hearkening to His People

have been moved by anything in religion, still if you were really convinced of the love of Jesus, as surely as water flowed from the smitten rock, so surely would love to Jesus flow from your rocky heart.

Now if there were no other view of Christ but this, then love to Jesus would be the only mark of a believer. The love of the Lord and not the fear of the Lord would be the sum of all wisdom. But there is another view of Christ.

Could I again lift away the veil of unbelief that covers your eyes and show unto you the loving Saviour, your first question would be, Why is He a bleeding Saviour? Why these pierced hands and feet? Why that pierced side and bleeding brow? Why is He a man of sorrows and acquainted with grief? Why does God save sinners in this awful way and not in another way?

Ah! my friends, could I convince you that the reason is that God is first a holy God, even in forgiving; could I show you that God has given us a law which demands perfect obedience; that His curse lies upon all and all are under the curse; that God hath made His own Son a curse for us; that we believing on Him might escape that curse; could I show you that God is just while He justifies the believer; could I show you that by laying on Christ the iniquities of us all, He is more plainly seen to be holy than if He had cast all men into hell – if I could show you all this, then I know you would go away from this great sight filled with most solemn thoughts. You would rejoice with trembling: 'Our God is a consuming fire; fearful in praises, doing wonders. Surely I am fearfully and wonderfully saved.'

A new feeling would thus spring up in your bosom. The feelings of love would still be there, but now the feeling of awe would mingle with it. And just as you may have seen two streams, one calm and clear, the other rapid and violent, meeting together and blending their waters to form one majestic river flowing onward to the ocean, so do the temper of love and the temper of awful reverence meet and blend together in the believer's bosom, to form the one majestic stream of holy fear, flowing toward the Lord our God. This is the fear of the Lord which is the sum of all true wisdom. This is the temper of those of whom the prophet speaks.

2. THEY THINK UPON HIS NAME.

This is a genuine mark of the true believer. There is no law of our nature more sure than that by which the affections regulate and draw after them the thoughts. Upon whatever object the affections are fixed, there the mind works with by far the greatest power and the greatest frequency.

When you can fix the affection of a child upon the subject which he is learning, you must often have remarked, how easily it is learned. The affections hurry on the mind toward the object and even his dreams will be filled with thoughts of what he loves. So it is with full-grown men: where the treasure is, there the heart is, and where the heart is, there the thoughts are. When a well-beloved child is in a distant land, who can tell how often a mother's heart will almost involuntarily lead her to think of her absent boy? Just so it is with the believer, with one who has found more than father, mother, sister, brother, in Christ, one who has been enlightened to see Jesus as altogether lovely. Here too the heart that loves the Lord will often draw the thoughts away to Him whom, having not seen, he loves.

Do you object that the believer cannot be always thinking of his Lord? The world and its concerns must often take up all his mind. I answer, True, neither can the mother be always thinking of her absent boy. The world and its concerns must often occupy all her mind, but in the one case as surely as in the other, there is felt in the busiest hours the pulling of affection, as if it would fain draw the mind away to things more beloved. And there are, ever and anon, when the affections hurry the soul away to distant scenes, glimpses like the openings in a cloudy sky when the blue heaven is displayed. These are sweet and sudden risings of soul away from the tame and dull monotony of things present. The heart of the believer has sudden dartings of faith and ejaculatory prayer even in the busiest hours which draw down glimpses of the reconciled countenance of God and lift off half the burden of the world. And when all work is done, when the busy hours of day are over, then does the loving soul hasten away to the object of its love, the mother sits down to think and speak about her boy, the believer communes with his own heart upon his bed and is still; he meditates upon Jesus in the night watches.

Oh! my friends, if you know not what it is habitually, intently, joyfully to think upon His Name in the multitude of your thoughts within you, then you know not what it is to love Jesus. You know not what it is to be in Jesus. You are not one of His.

3. THE TIME SPOKEN OF.

'*Then* they that feared the Lord spake often.' To ascertain the force of the word THEN we must read the preceding verses. And here we find that it was a time of great wickedness and profanity, especially in speaking stout words against God.

In looking through the Bible we find that blasphemy or speaking stout words against God, against Christ, and against the people of Christ, has always abounded most in the wickedest times. Looking as far back as Enoch, the seventh from Adam, we find him, in his short prophecy recorded by Jude, marking this as the great sin of his day. 'Behold, the Lord cometh with ten thousands of his saints, to execute judgment upon all, and to convince all that are ungodly among them of all their ungodly deeds which they have ungodly committed, and of all their hard speeches which ungodly sinners have spoken against him' (*Jude* 14–15).

Our Lord Himself bore witness to the same thing in the days of His flesh when, rebuking the Pharisees, He said, 'O generation of vipers, how can ye, being evil, speak good things?' (*Matt.* 12:34). And Paul tells us the same thing of the natural man in his day, 'Their throat is an open sepulchre; with their tongues they have used deceit; the poison of asps is under their lips: whose mouth is full of cursing and bitterness' (*Rom.* 3:13).

And just such was the generation with which Malachi had to contend. It was a time when men spoke stout words against God and against the people of God. It is vain to serve God they said, and what profit is it that we have kept His ordinances and that we have walked mournfully before the Lord of hosts? They here try to cast contempt upon the ordinances of God, upon the reading of the Word, upon fasts and sacraments. And now they say, we call the proud happy; yea, they that work wickedness are set up; yea, they that tempt God are even delivered. Here they cast out insinuations against the people of God because they are often afflicted, because all the day long they have been plagued and chastened every morning, whilst the wicked often spread and flourish like the green bay tree. Surely, say they, it is better to be wicked, it is better to tempt God, and then we shall be delivered. Poor souls, they did not know that these light afflictions of the believer, which are but for a moment, are working out for him an exceeding weight of eternal glory.

Now my friends, it was then, when the wicked were becoming stout against God, when blasphemy was rising high to heaven, when

The Lord Hearkening to His People

the wicked spoke contemptuously of the children of God, it was then they that feared the Lord spoke often one to another. You would have thought perhaps that when the wicked became loud and clamorous and open in speaking out their hard speeches, that then the people of Christ would have been scattered and desolate, as the sheep are all scattered when they hear the cry of the wolves. But no, that is the very time when they hold fastest together and speak often one to another. When you pour oil upon the troubled waters you might suppose that the waves by their violence would soon dilute and disperse it, but no, the more the waves rage, the more closely do the drops of oil cling together, keeping more and more separate from the water.

Ah! my friends, our day is just Malachi's day once again. Now is the time when the enemies of God are waxing valiant, when their cry is getting louder, when they speak stout words against God, against His worship, against His ministers, against His people. How often nowadays do the calm, quiet valleys which seem made by God for retirement for prayer and praise, resound with the profanity of the Sabbath-breaker. And the stillness of your quiet hamlet on a summer's evening, how often is it broken by the loud cries of the scoffer, and the deep curses of the swearer. Oh! how many on every hand are saying, 'It is vain to serve God, and what profit should we have if we were to keep His ordinances?' How many are doing the devil's work, tempting the young and inexperienced, calling the proud happy and slandering and scoffing at the people of God?

Come my friends, ye can discern the face of the sky and can ye not discern the signs of the times? Now, then, is the time for all that fear the Lord and love to think upon His name, not to shrink away and be scattered like timid sheep on the mountains, but to draw closer one to another. They should open their hearts more to one another; they should give counsel and take counsel one of another.

This is God's way of dealing. He suffers the hell-hounds of slander and blasphemy to be let loose for a season, just so that all who love the Lord Jesus may cling far closer to Christ and cling far closer to one another. As it was then, so let it be now. When the enemies of God speak loudest, then let the people of God speak oftenest one to another.

4. THEY SPOKE OFTEN TO ONE ANOTHER.

i. They Did So to Keep Their Own Souls Alive.

When iniquity abounds, then the love of many waxes cold. And that man is no believer at all who does not look abroad upon such a season with anxiety for his own soul lest it be frozen up. It is insensibility and not courage to be unmoved by great danger, it is a sign of death or deathlike slumber to be still and sleep when the snow and frost are setting fiercely in, instead of using every means of resistance. And just so, if there be one of you who thinks himself a believer and yet does not feel himself roused to use every means of resisting the influence of abounding iniquity, it is plain that you have only a name to live while you are dead.

The man who has truly come to Christ and has found peace in believing has laid aside all high thoughts of himself. He is one who knows that his heart is deceitful above all things, utterly incapable of resisting temptations, of bearing out against the allurements or the scoffs of the world. And if there were no such saying as, 'Greater is he that is in you, than he that is in the world', he would utterly despair of holding up his head, or of keeping his garments clean in this ungodly world.

But he knows that there is an Almighty Spirit promised to all believers, and that that Spirit works never without means, always by means, and therefore does he cling earnestly to the simplest and weakest means which God may bless. He sits down at the feet of a child if that child is a child of God. He will learn from a mere babe if that babe can tell him of Christ. Not once or twice but often will he go and commune eye to eye and soul with soul. This is the temper of every believer. This was the temper of the mighty Paul when writing to the Romans. They were but babes in knowledge, yet he professes his anxiety to come to them, not for their sakes only, but for his own sake also, 'that I may be comforted together with you by the mutual faith both of you and me'. Think of Paul the apostle sitting down to be comforted by the very men whom he was teaching, and then see one grand reason why 'they that fear the Lord' should 'speak often one to another'.

ii. THEY DID SO TO KEEP ALIVE THE SOULS OF FELLOW BELIEVERS. The first cry of the awakened Paul was, 'Lord, what wilt thou have me to do?' And just so it is with every true believer in Jesus. He cannot remain at rest without doing something for Christ. What poor shall I feed? What soul shall I visit? What ignorant ones shall I teach? This is the cry of every genuine believer. Now, though the Lord is seldom slow in pointing out some peculiar corner of his vineyard for the converted soul to occupy, and his having already given the good will to work is a plain evidence that he will shortly open up work for that soul to do, still believing minds do often put the question, What would the Lord have me to do?

How plain, how open, how cheering a field this Scripture opens up in these days of trouble and rebuke and blasphemy! Let them that love the Lord speak often one to another. Let us consider one another, how to provoke one another to love and to good works, not forsaking the assembling of ourselves together as the manner of some is, but exhorting one another and so much more as we see (by the signs of the times) that the day is approaching.

Here is a wide field for you to cultivate. Oh! converted soul! Support the weak, nourish babes, breathe the gentle word of consolation into the ear of the mourner. Speak gentle words of rebuke to them that are going backward. Oh! believers, ye are members one of another, and if one member be hurt, the whole body should be grieved. If one member be honoured all should rejoice along with it.

What shall we say then of those companies where those who are called Christians meet and yet Christ is not spoken of? What shall we say of those scenes of merriment which those called Christians frequent, and yet Christ is not the subject of their joy? Ah! my friends, 'An enemy hath done this.'

The very instrument which God hath chosen to be the safeguard of believers, the devil is turning into an engine to drag them down to hell. The very seasons of social meeting which God intended believers to use in helping one another heavenward, in preening one another's feathers for a higher flight above the scoffs and the scowls of a blaspheming world, these very seasons the devil has perverted to seasons of hateful conformity to the world, to cover with pitch the believer's wings. Truly one dead fly spoils the whole pot of ointment.

Oh! my believing friends, awake from this horrid profanation. Let not Satan rob you of this precious means of grace. But while the world grows louder and louder in speaking stout words against God, let believers cling closer and closer on to one another, leave the world to talk of the heathen and Christless things.

Let believers listen to the Word of the Lord, 'Come, my people, enter thou into thy chambers, and shut thy doors about thee: hide thyself as it were for a little moment, until the indignation be overpast' (*Isa.* 26:20).

5. HOW THE LORD RESPONDED.

i. *'The* LORD *hearkened, and heard it, and a book of remembrance was written before Him for them that feared the* LORD, *and that thought upon his name.'*

This is the very same blessing which Jesus promises in the New Testament, 'Where two or three are gathered together in my name, there am I in the midst of them', to bless them and to do them good. 'Lo I am with you alway, even unto the end of the world.' Most gracious declarations! No true believers can meet but Jesus is there. He hearkens, actually bends His ear to hear the words of counsel or encouragement or rebuke or mutual faith that pass from lip to lip. He hears every word. He records it all. A book is written before Him and every sweet word of faith, of love, of joy, of encouragement, is treasured up there and shall be read before an assembled universe.

Yes, the weakest words, if only words of faith, are precious in the sight of God. When the believer looks back over a well-spent day, when he asks his own heart how many words he hath spoken for Christ, he may often be apt to think that he has laboured for naught and in vain. But no! He that numbers the hairs of his head, has numbered, yea, written down all the gracious words of his lips. The words breathed in the darkness of a sick-room; the words of encouragement spoken to some despairing believer; his chance words by the wayside; the very looks of Christian sympathy which he exchanged. All these are chronicled and shall, in that day, be greatly rewarded.

Ah, then, worldly-talking believers, if such a character can be, Christians who lack the speech of Canaan, what record can that hearkening Lord draw up of your daily conversations? Ah! well did James say, 'If any man offend not in word, the same is a perfect man.'

Awake believers to know that you are bought with a price, not your souls only but your tongues also. See then that your conversation be always with grace, seasoned with salt.

ii. *'I will spare them, as a man spareth his own son that serveth him.'*

I put this next because it plainly relates to God's treatment of them in this world. Tell me, any one who is a father, tell me how it is you deal with your own son that serveth you, and then I will tell you how God deals peculiarly with those believers who speak often one to another.

Oh! how tenderly does not an earthly father deal with his own son? He clothes him, he feeds him, he shall never want any good thing. If it is needful to correct him, he does it in measure and in love, for what son is he whom the father chasteneth not? He is the heir and therefore the father gives all things into his hand. So does God with his own. Justified by faith, we are His own children. He puts the Spirit of adoption in us that we may serve Him, saying, 'Abba, Father.' He works in us love that we may be partakers of His holiness. And as we are the heirs, He says to us, 'All things are yours.'

iii. *'And they shall be mine, saith the* LORD *of hosts, in that day when I make up my jewels.'*

The great day is at hand when God will make up His jewels. Those who know anything of the art of jewellery know that the arranging in order, the cutting and setting of the jewels, is a task of peculiar nicety, requiring particular taste and skilfulness, whether the jewels are to be made up into rings or crowns.

But the Lord Himself will, in that day, arrange His own people who, on earth, spoke often one to another. And just as it will be one great curse of the wicked to be bound up in bundles like the tares to be burned, they that have smothered one another's convictions and helped one another to hell, to curse one another everlastingly, so shall it be one great blessedness of believers, who on earth helped one another's faith, to speak often one to another in heaven, helping one another's joy.

They that have been jewels together amid the scoffs of a scoffing world shall be jewels set together everlastingly in the crown of their Saviour.